John Wayne

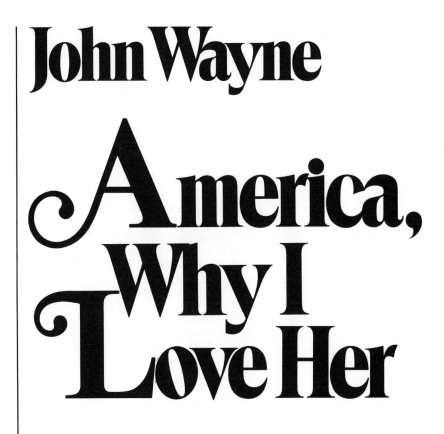

America, Why I Love Her

with

Billy Liebert and John Mitchum

 Simon and Schuster, New York

Published by Simon and Schuster
A Division of Gulf & Western Corporation
Simon & Schuster Building
Rockefeller Center
1230 Avenue of the Americas
New York, New York 10020

Photo editor: Vincent Virga
Designed by Libra Graphics, Inc.
Manufactured in the United States of America
Printed by The Murray Printing Company, Inc.
Bound by The Book Press, Inc.
1   2   3   4   5   6   7   8   9   10

Library of Congress Cataloging in Publication Data
Liebert, Billy.
    America, why I love her.

    Monologues with piano acc.; includes chord symbols.
    Words principally by J. Mitchum and H. Barnes; in-
troductions by J. Wayne.
    Words also printed as text on p.
    CONTENTS: Why I love her.—The hyphen.—Mis raíces
están aquí (My roots are buried here) [etc.]
    1. Monologues with music (Piano)   2. Patriotic
music, American.   I. Wayne, John, 1907-
II. Mitchum, John. America, why I love her.
III. Barnes, Howard, 1913-   America, why I love her.
IV. Title.
M1626.L [M1629]   784.7′19′73   77-21712

ISBN 0-671-22313-5
ISBN 0-671-22314-3 deluxe

Contents

Foreword

In writing the foreword to this book, I would like very much to say a word or two about the people you will see credited as having contributed to its music and its prose. I've worked with these people for some time now, and the simplest way I can say what I want to say is that, to a man, they have participated because they all have a profound reverence for America. Just as I do, they state that without the two hundred years of this great nation's existence, the poetry, the music and the thoughts in this book could never have been written.

Therefore, let me say that we who have contributed to this book feel it is a dedication to all of you readers from us who salute all that has gone before and eagerly await whatever lies ahead.

JOHN WAYNE

Why I Love Her

YOU ask me "Why I Love Her"? Well, I think it's pretty well explained with the words and music, but we can dwell a little more on it.

"From the mountains" (and we sure have them). The Adirondacks, the Catskills, the Cascades and the Great Smokies. The Grand Tetons, the Bitterroots, the Allegheny and the Blue Ridge. And let's not forget our Spanish sisters, the Sierra Madres and the Sierra Nevadas, and of course the big daddy of them all, the Rockies. No one in a lifetime could explore them all and I can't help but think of a few lines from a great song by Bob Nolan that the "Sons of the Pioneers" sing.

The desert breeze that brushed my hair,
The leaf that fell from who knows where,
The scent of wild flowers in the air,
Is just the touch of God's hand.

"To the prairie." Well, if you look westward from a Kansas prairie along about evening, you'll be amazed at what God can do with a sunset. Take a slow ride through Nebraska, stand in a field of tall Iowa corn or sample the cheeses of Wisconsin. Michigan, Indiana, Illinois and Ohio—names and places that spring from some of the richest soil in our known world. Rivers like the Ohio and the wide Missouri funnel their waters into the mighty Mississippi, which in turn carries much of the bountiful prairie harvest to a needy world. Rivers like the Cumberland, the Osage, the Platte.

The settlements that sprang into cities because of rivers such as those are a pulsating heart of America: St. Louis, St. Paul, Natchez, Omaha, Louisville and New Orleans. Their names are a part of our heritage and they grow stronger with each passing year.

"To the oceans, white with foam." The Oregon Coast—unforgettable—awe-inspiring during a winter storm. Massachusetts, with its Marblehead and Martha's Vineyard. And how about rip-roaring, always-moving New York City? The Eastern shore with Delaware and its apple orchards making you wish

you were a kid again. The pine forests of North Carolina and the southern peaches of Georgia. Seems to me that they still set beauty standards all over the world.

Watch a Hawaiian island sunrise from the old Lahaina Inn or Maui. Go ahead! Dream of old whalers and island kĭngs! In this country you're free to go any place you want to go. From the Florida Keys to Alaska, from Hawaii to Maine, Americans move freely within her border and there's no one going to stop you.

Sure you have to pay your dues—but walleyed pike are waiting for you in Minnesota; backpacking for free in Washington, and watermelon's ripe and juicy in Mississippi. Dig for oysters in Maryland or go after steelhead in Idaho. Try shooting the rapids on the Colorado or picking blueberries in Maine.

Try your country on for size. It's free and it's a big order. I've been doing it for years and I can never get enough of America.

Why I Love Her

Words by
JOHN MITCHUM
ASCAP

Music arranged and adapted by
BILLY LIEBERT
ASCAP

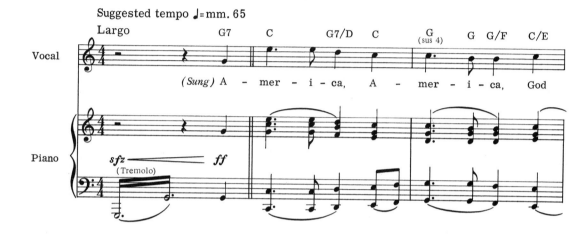

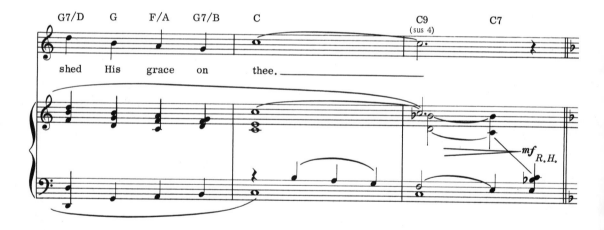

And do you think of them when you stroll along a New York City dock? Have you seen a snowflake

drifting in the Rockies, way up high? Have you seen the sun come blazing down from a

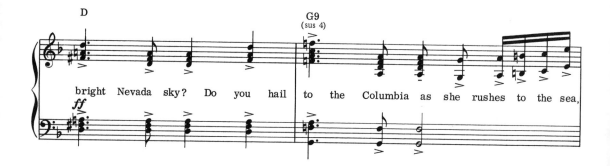

bright Nevada sky? Do you hail to the Columbia as she rushes to the sea,

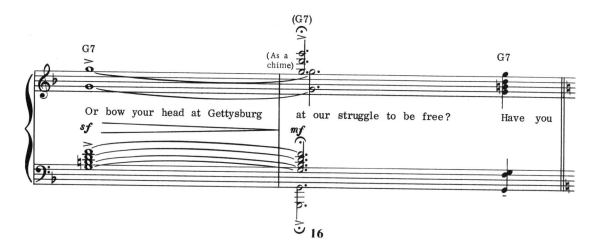

Or bow your head at Gettysburg at our struggle to be free? Have you

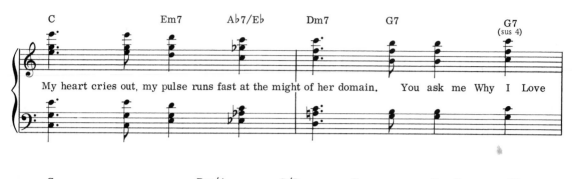

My heart cries out, my pulse runs fast at the might of her domain.   You ask me Why I Love

(Sung) And

Her? I've a million reasons why: My beautiful America, beneath God's wide, wide sky.

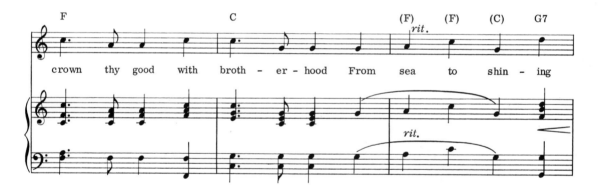

crown thy good with broth - er - hood From sea to shin - ing

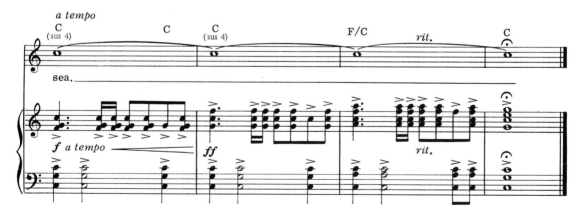

sea.

"America, America, God shed his grace on thee . . ."

You ask me Why I Love Her? Well, give me time and I'll
    explain.
Have you seen a Kansas sunset or an Arizona rain?
Have you drifted on a bayou down Louisiana way?
Have you watched a cold fog drifting over San Francisco Bay?

Have you heard a bobwhite calling in the Carolina pines,
Or heard the bellow of a diesel at the Appalachia mines?
Does the call of Niagara thrill you when you hear her
    waters roar?
Do you look with awe and wonder at her Massachusetts shore,
Where men who braved a hard new world first stepped on
    Plymouth's rock?
And do you think of them when you stroll along a New York
    City dock?

Have you seen a snowflake drifting in the Rockies, way up
    high?
Have you seen the sun come blazing down from a bright Nevada
    sky?
Do you hail to the Columbia as she rushes to the sea,
Or bow your head at Gettysburg at our struggle to be free?

Have you seen the mighty Tetons? Have you watched an
    eagle soar?
Have you seen the Mississippi roll along Missouri's shore?
Have you felt a chill at Michigan when on a winter's day
Her waters rage along the shore in thunderous display?
Does the word "Aloha" make you warm? Do you stare in
    disbelief
When you see the surf come roaring in at Waimea Reef?

From Alaska's cold to the Everglades, from the Rio Grande
    to Maine,
My heart cries out, my pulse runs fast at the might of
    her domain.
You ask me Why I Love Her? I've a million reasons why:
My beautiful America, beneath God's wide, wide sky.

    "And crown thy good with brotherhood
      From sea to shining sea."

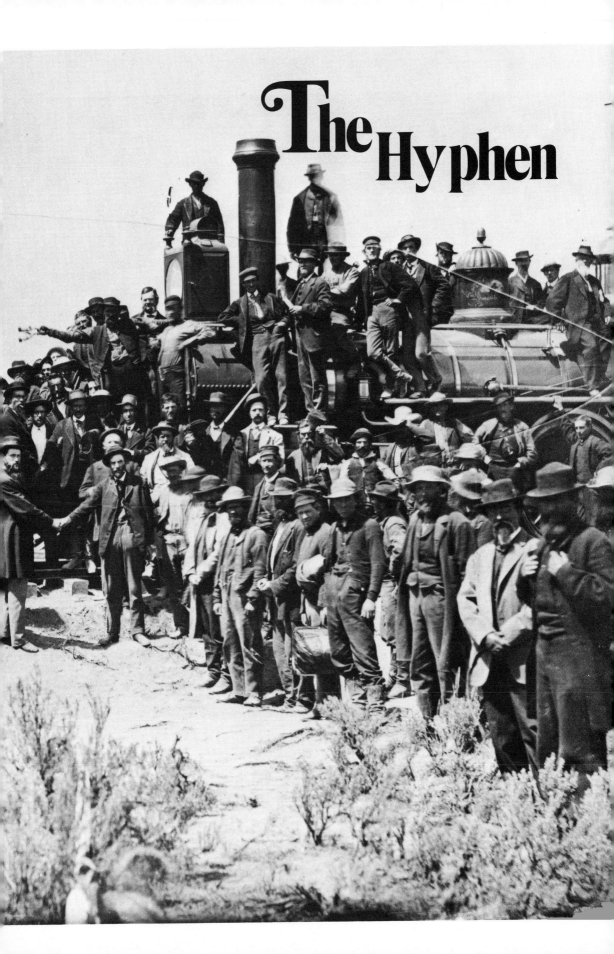

The Hyphen

24

EVERYONE knows by now that America is made up of every race, color and creed under the sun. The inscription on the base of the Statue of Liberty is for real: "From her beacon-hand flows world-wide welcome."

Each succeeding wave of immigrants had a tough row to hoe, that's for sure! When the potato famine of 1846 devastated Ireland, thousands of Irishmen flocked to our shores. They were greeted by signs in Boston, Philadelphia and New York that spelled out the message that "no Irish need apply" and those men fanned out across the nation in search of honest toil. And yet a descendant of those Irishmen became the thirty-fifth President of the United States.

Our country stands today as the world's oldest living Republic. We are the greatest sociological experiment that the world has ever known. If we fail our trust, Democracy fails.

Like Ireland, the Middle East has long been divided by ancient hatreds, hatreds that have no place on our shores. Religious wars and fierce ideological conflicts should never be a part of America; people came to Her to escape religious and political persecution. Sure, we've had our problems. What family doesn't? But they haven't stopped us. The total divisiveness that has burdened many other nations hasn't caught on here. We have our disagreements, but let some other country step on our tail and they'll find out how quickly Americans become united.

Each day that goes by seems to make us gel a little more. Maybe it's because each group of people who came here has given us their tastes in food and in music, their skills in art and designs and the customs of their lands. But more important, they brought with them an intense desire for freedom.

Where else in the world can you get a good hamburger sandwich, a cheese blintz, a taco or some real lasagne all in the same block? And what would an early morning call or a cold mountain location be like without some good hot coffee topped off with some Danish pastry or German strudel?

Where else in the world can you get Chopin études, Dixieland jazz or Country Western music just by twisting your radio dials? It's hard to remember that bluegrass fiddling is a direct descendant of Scottish bagpipes. And give credit to Peter Tchaikovsky when you hear "Tonight We Love." It is his music.

So bring your recipe for good Irish stew with you, but leave bigotry and hatred behind. Sing and dance to the balalaika but bring no walls with you. Praise God anyway you so desire. Just allow your neighbor the same right. For each person you see has the same needs that you do. We all want respect, concern, and yes, love.

When we all tear down the walls of bigotry and prejudice and live in real harmony with ourselves and others, then we'll all say "I am an American," pure and simple. And "The Hyphen" will no longer apply to any of us. When that day comes, the world can count on us for another ten thousand years, for we'll be a brighter, a stronger and an *undivided* America.

The Hyphen

Words by
JOHN MITCHUM and
HOWARD BARNES
ASCAP

Music by
BILLY LIEBERT and
LES TAYLOR
ASCAP

(Spoken)

The Hyphen, Webster's Dictionary defines,
Is a symbol used to divide a compound word or a single word.
So it seems to me that when a man calls himself
An "Afro-American," a "Mexican-American," "Italian-
  American," an "Irish-American," "Jewish-American,"
What he's sayin' is, "I'm a divided American."

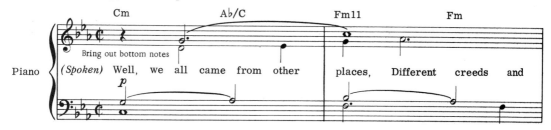

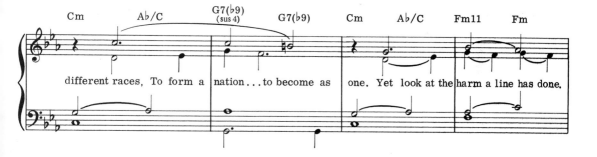

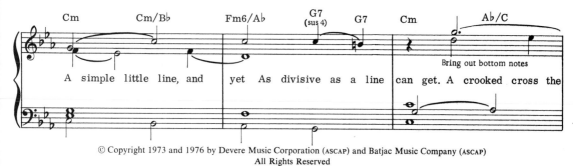

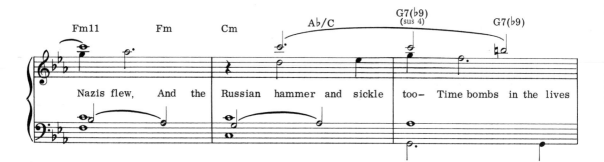

Nazis flew, And the Russian hammer and sickle too— Time bombs in the lives

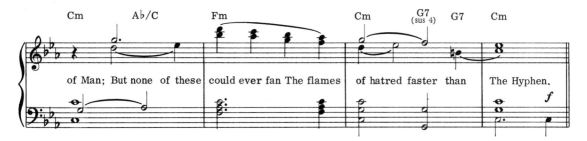

of Man; But none of these could ever fan The flames of hatred faster than The Hyphen.

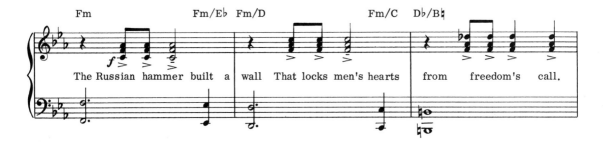

The Russian hammer built a wall That locks men's hearts from freedom's call.

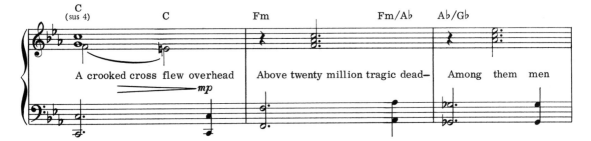

A crooked cross flew overhead Above twenty million tragic dead— Among them men

from this great nation, Who died for freedom's preservation. A hyphen is

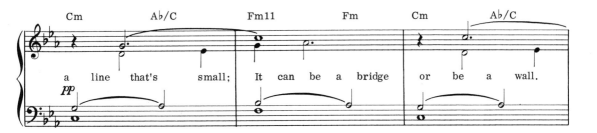

a line that's small; It can be a bridge or be a wall.

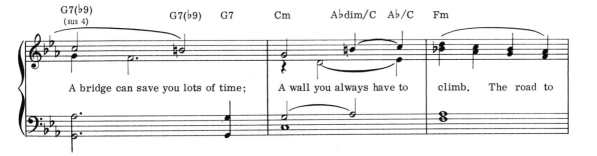

A bridge can save you lots of time; A wall you always have to climb. The road to

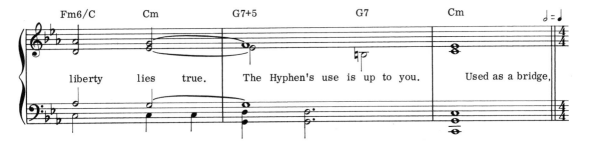

liberty lies true. The Hyphen's use is up to you. Used as a bridge,

Lo stesso tempo

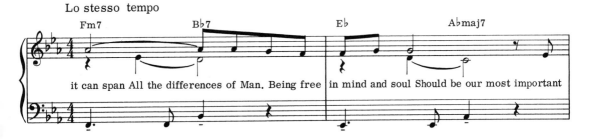

it can span All the differences of Man. Being free in mind and soul Should be our most important

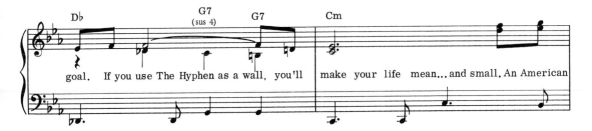

goal. If you use The Hyphen as a wall, you'll make your life mean...and small. An American

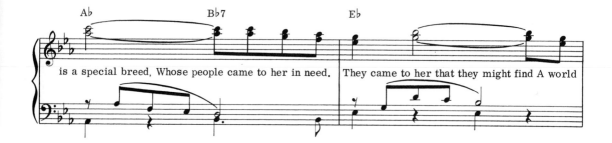

is a special breed, Whose people came to her in need. They came to her that they might find A world

where they'd have peace of mind, Where men are equal...and something more —
Stand taller than they stood before.

So you be wise in your decision, And that little line won't cause division. Let's join hands with one

another... For in this land, each man's your brother. United we stand... divided we fall...

We're Americans... and that says it all.

The Hyphen, Webster's Dictionary defines,
Is a symbol used to divide a compound word or a single word.
So it seems to me that when a man calls himself
An "Afro-American," a "Mexican-American," "Italian-
          American,"
An "Irish-American," "Jewish-American,"
What he's sayin' is, "I'm a divided American."

Well, we all came from other places,
Different creeds and different races,
To form a nation . . . to become as one.
Yet look at the harm a line has done—
A simple little line, and yet
As divisive as a line can get.
A crooked cross the Nazis flew,
And the Russian hammer and sickle too—
Time bombs in the lives of Man;
But none of these could ever fan
The flames of hatred faster than
The Hyphen.

The Russian hammer built a wall
That locks men's hearts from freedom's call.
A crooked cross flew overhead
Above twenty million tragic dead—
Among them men from this great nation,
Who died for freedom's preservation.
A hyphen is a line that's small;
It can be a bridge or be a wall.
A bridge can save you lots of time;
A wall you always have to climb.
The road to liberty lies true.
The Hyphen's use is up to you.

Used as a bridge, it can span
All the differences of Man.
Being free in mind and soul
Should be our most important goal.
If you use The Hyphen as a wall,
You'll make your life mean . . . and small.
An American is a special breed,
Whose people came to her in need.
They came to her that they might find
A world where they'd have peace of mind,
Where men are equal . . . and something more—
Stand taller than they stood before.

So you be wise in your decision,
And that little line won't cause division.
Let's join hands with one another . . .
For in this land, each man's your brother.
United we stand . . . divided we fall.
We're Americans . . . and that says it all.

Mis Raíces Están Aquí

(My Roots Are Buried Here)

FOR me to deny a lifelong love of the West would be impossible. There's an old saying that states, "You can take the boy out of the country, but you can't take the country out of the boy." I know good and well that it applies to me.

In the last forty years I've ridden over a lot of territory on horseback and from up close you can see just how tough the southwest deserts can be. The ancient Arizona mountains have been worn down by blowing winds for tens of thousands of years, while the rugged peaks of New Mexico's Organ mountains stand like bleak sentinels against the clear blue sky.

For hundreds of years, people with the blood of the Aztecs in their veins have lived and died on that harsh, yet beautiful land and names like El Paso, Las Cruces, Alamogordo, Santa Fe, Del Rio and Nogales are perpetual monuments to their being there.

Now over twenty million Americans look back on that proud heritage. The colorful vaqueros who herded cattle on that once savage land, faced 120 degree heat with the same determination that brought them through bitter winter winds that could freeze men's souls. Their quiet pride and dignity, springing from their love of the land, made fearful hardships seem easy and their way of life that kept them away from hubs of civilization for months at a time gave them an inner resourcefulness that has made their way of life seem a romantic legend. The dons and the Caballeros were among the first settlers in the West and have left their mark indelibly upon it.

Yes, Americans are a special breed of people, all walks of life, and yet, all as one. Today a city dweller is amazed to find people living many miles from the nearest town in remote ranches that are swallowed up by the vastness of the West. Colorado, Montana, Wyoming, New Mexico, Arizona and Utah are all places with pasts so rich in history they defy description. Yet all of those ranchers and their wives and children take hardship as a matter of course. I've known men personally who have gone to the high country to check their cattle, been caught in a blizzard and had to fend for themselves for a week or more at a time. When the weather abated enough to let them get back to their homes, the first question asked of them would be "How are the cattle holding out?" and more often than not the answer would be a laconic "Fine."

When spring would come and the high mountains gave off their precious horde of cool snow water, fragile desert flowers would bloom and the soft desert nights would be filled with their scent. Guitars would round out the night sounds and coyotes would add their voices to the chorus.

Then the men of the West would count their blessings in that eternal land. Leave their way of life? Never! *Mis raíces están aquí!* My roots are buried here!

Mis Raíces Están Aquí
(My Roots Are Buried Here)

Words by
JOHN MITCHUM
ASCAP

Music by
BILLY LIEBERT
ASCAP

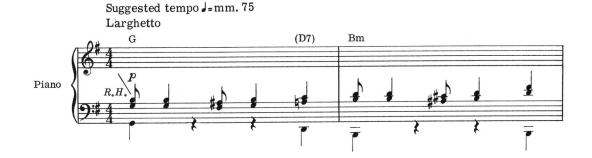

Suggested tempo ♩=mm. 75
Larghetto

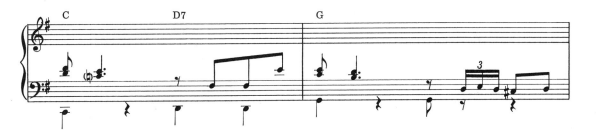

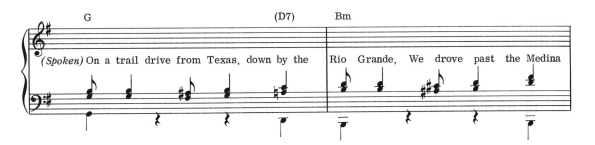

(Spoken) On a trail drive from Texas, down by the Rio Grande, We drove past the Medina

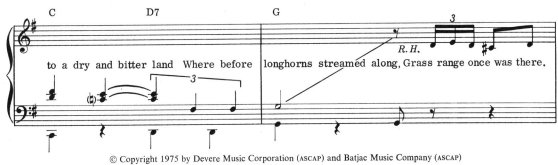

to a dry and bitter land Where before longhorns streamed along, Grass range once was there.

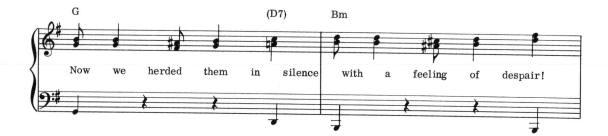

Now we herded them in silence with a feeling of despair!

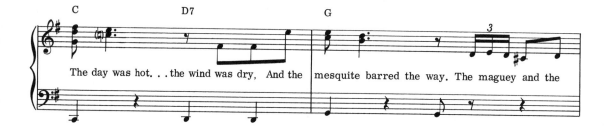

The day was hot. . .the wind was dry, And the mesquite barred the way. The maguey and the

cactus tried to drain our lives away. We came up to a ranch house dying in the

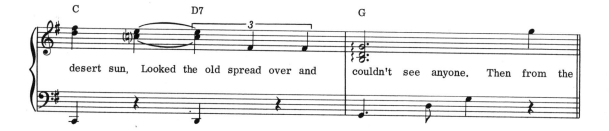

desert sun, Looked the old spread over and couldn't see anyone. Then from the

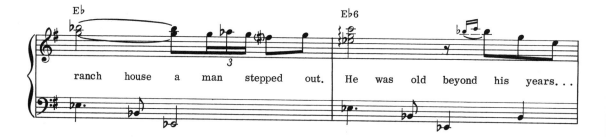

ranch house a man stepped out. He was old beyond his years...

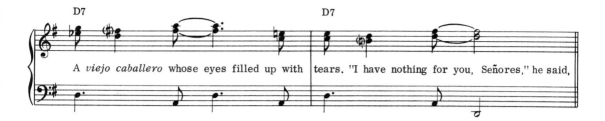

A *viejo caballero* whose eyes filled up with tears. "I have nothing for you, Señores," he said,

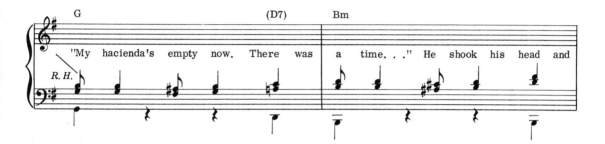

"My hacienda's empty now. There was a time..." He shook his head and

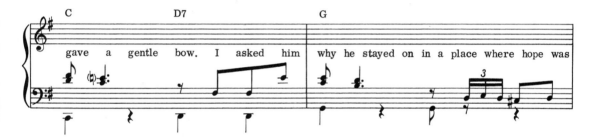

gave a gentle bow. I asked him why he stayed on in a place where hope was

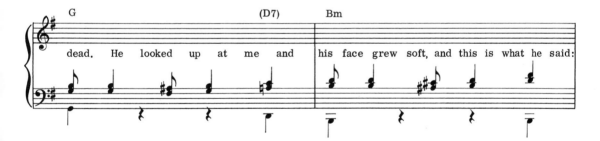

dead. He looked up at me and his face grew soft, and this is what he said:

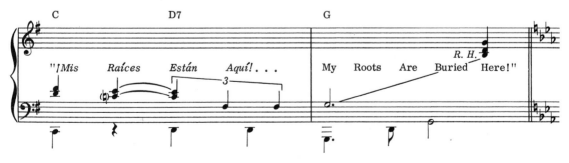

"¡Mis Raíces Están Aquí!... My Roots Are Buried Here!"

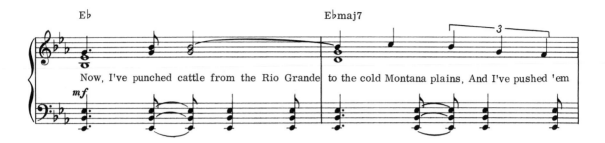

Now, I've punched cattle from the Rio Grande to the cold Montana plains, And I've pushed 'em

through New Mexico and through Arizona rains. I've seen ranchers hanging on when it's been

forty-five below—And the thought's always crossed my mind as to why they just don't go

To a place where life is easier and where nature's not so hard. . . And then the

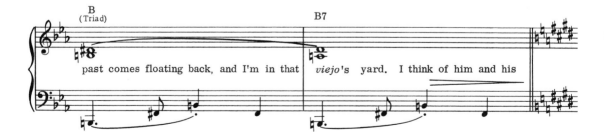

past comes floating back, and I'm in that *viejo's* yard. I think of him and his

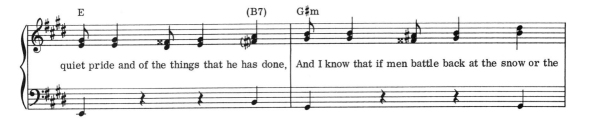

quiet pride and of the things that he has done, | And I know that if men battle back at the snow or the

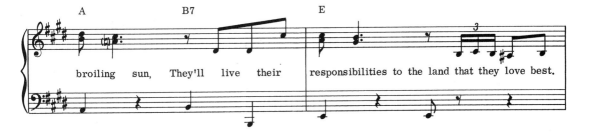

broiling sun, They'll live their | responsibilities to the land that they love best.

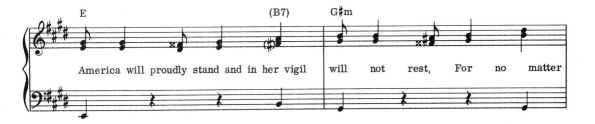

America will proudly stand and in her vigil | will not rest, For no matter

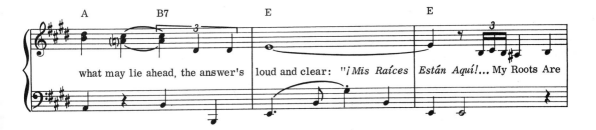

what may lie ahead, the answer's | loud and clear: *"¡ Mis Raíces Están Aquí!... My Roots Are*

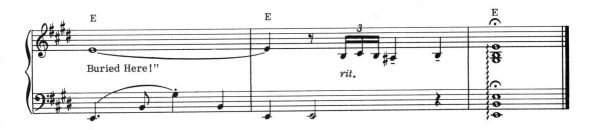

Buried Here!" | *rit.*

On a trail drive from Texas, down by the Rio Grande,
We drove past the Medina to a dry and bitter land
Where before the longhorns streamed along, grass range once
    was there.
Now we herded them in silence with a feeling of despair!

The day was hot . . . the wind was dry, and the mesquite barred
    the way.
The maguey and the cactus tried to drain our lives away.
We came up to a ranch house dying in the desert sun,
Looked the old spread over and couldn't see anyone.

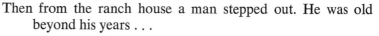

Then from the ranch house a man stepped out. He was old
    beyond his years . . .
A *viejo caballero* whose eyes filled up with tears.
"I have nothing for you, Señores," he said. "My hacienda's
    empty now.
There was a time . . ." He shook his head and gave a
    gentle bow.
I asked him why he'd stayed on in a place where
    hope was dead.
He looked up at me and his face grew soft, and this is
    what he said:
    "*¡Mis Raíces Están Aquí!* . . .
       My Roots Are Buried Here!"

Now, I've punched cattle from the Rio Grande to the
    cold Montana plains,
And I've pushed 'em through New Mexico and through
    Arizona rains.
I've seen ranchers hanging on when it's been forty-five below—
And the thought's always crossed my mind as to why they
    just don't go
To a place where life is easier and where nature's not
    so hard . . .
And then the past comes floating back, and I'm in that
    viejo's yard.
I think of him and his quiet pride and of the things that
    he has done,
And I know that if men battle back at the snow or the
    broiling sun,
They'll live their responsibilities to the land that they love best.
America will proudly stand and in her vigil will not rest,
For no matter what may lie ahead, the answer's loud and clear:
    "*¡Mis Raíces Están Aquí!* . . .
       My Roots Are Buried Here!"

The People

ALFRED STIEGLITZ, *The Steerage*. 1907. PHOTOGRAVURE FROM *Camera Work*, 1911. COLLECTION, THE MUSEUM OF MODERN ART, NEW YORK

IN THE latter 1930's a man named Adolf Hitler proclaimed that the Germans were the "master race" and would eventually rule the world. On a warm June night in 1938 a sharecropper's son who had made his way from the fields of Alabama to Madison Square Garden gave Americans a thrill lost forever to those who missed that night. That boy was Joseph Louis Barrow, the Brown Bomber. He stepped into the ring against the pride of the German Army, and in less than three minutes he destroyed Hitler's myth forever. And the free world went wild.

Israel Baline came to America from Russia and no one really noticed that fact until he changed his name to Irving Berlin. It seems like he's been here forever. There's one thing we know for sure, his songs will be.

Fabens, Texas, brought a young man into the world in August of 1931. He didn't grow too much physically but he sure has topped his world in stature. Right now he's had about seven thousand winners in thoroughbred racing. My! Mother Shoemaker, you must be proud of your young son Willy.

America has so much talent running around loose, that name dropping is easy. Who can forget the long range clutch passing of Johnny Unitas, the sandlot kid from Pittsburgh? How many people, would you say, hum a Cole Porter tune at one time or another? What American lives who never heard of John Denver or Frank Sinatra?

I look back on December 7, 1941, Pearl Harbor. Our Pacific Fleet was destroyed, our Air Force reduced to rubble. The call went out to all of us to get busy, to roll up our shirtsleeves and get things moving. Our factories poured out in less than two years the most formidable fleet and the biggest Air Force in the world. And all of this came about because of the men and women of America working together in a common cause. Unheralded people, your friends and neighbors who may never have stepped on a concert stage or thrown a touchdown pass, but they built a monument to the awesome latent strength of America, and Hitler's and Hirohito's legions were destroyed.

All across our land are people who dedicate their lives to decency and compassion. Whenever a catastrophe strikes anywhere in the world, it seems that our people are among the first to send aid to the unfortunate victims of that catastrophe.

The farmers who drive their tractors along endless rows of cornfields or run giant wheat threshers across miles of golden grain work selflessly and in so doing strengthen our nation.

Millions of road miles pass under the wheels of our giant trucking industry and these drivers feel innately that they belong to America and America belongs to them. The people who work in and on Her soil are wedded to Her and they love Her.

In my fifty years of picture-making, I have been what some people might term a "star." Well, for my money, the stars in my crown are the people who lit the sets, groomed the stock, took the pictures and, in general, put the whole dad-blamed show on the road. People made me a star with blood, sweat and tears! And when it was needed, a prayer!

The People

Words by
JOHN MITCHUM and
HOWARD BARNES
ASCAP

Music by
BILLY LIEBERT
ASCAP

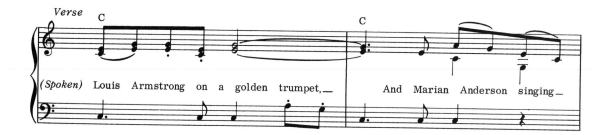

Verse

C

(Spoken) Louis Armstrong on a golden trumpet,— And Marian Anderson singing—

B♭ **G7** **G9** (sus 4)

"The Lord's Prayer"; — The savage power of Jack Dempsey,—

C **Fmaj9** **F**

And the quiet pride of Jesse Owens; — Merle Haggard

Em **Em7** **Fmaj7** **Gm** **A7** **Dm**

singing "Okie From Muskogee," — And Chet Atkins pickin' a guitar; — Bing Crosby at

G9 (sus 4) **F** **Em7 Dm C**

Christmastime,— And Charles Lindbergh crossing the Atlantic alone.—

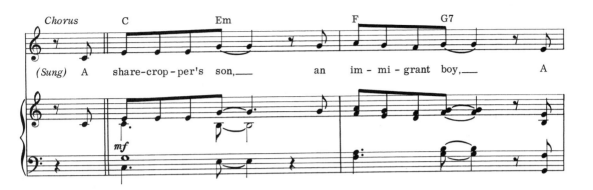

Chorus

(Sung) A share-crop-per's son,___ an im - mi - grant boy,___ A

ho - bo who rode all the rails,___ The mag - ic gui - tar of an

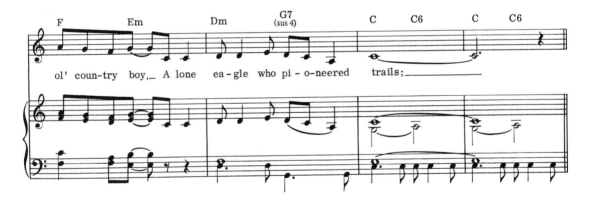

ol' coun-try boy,_ A lone ea-gle who pi - o-neered trails;___

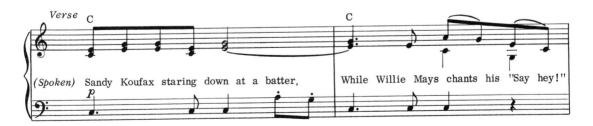

Verse

(Spoken) Sandy Koufax staring down at a batter, While Willie Mays chants his "Say hey!"

Maria Tallchief gliding in *Swan Lake,* ___ While Fred Astaire

dances on gossamer wings; ___ Billy Graham bringing God to millions,

And Jonas Salk bringing hope to the world; ___ Mahalia Jackson ___ closing her

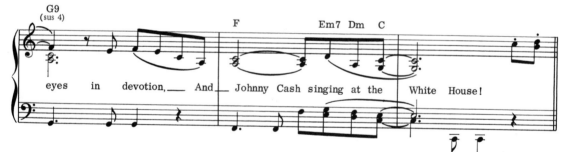

eyes in devotion, ___ And ___ Johnny Cash singing at the White House!

Chorus

(Sung) What makes the word "A - mer - i - ca" ring ___ With a sound that bright-ens the air? ___

54

It's peo-ple, her peo-ple, who have done their "own thing"— With

blood, sweat and tears, and a pray'r._____ *(Spoken)* Willie

Verse

Shoemaker booting Swaps home,__ While Eddie Arcaro wins the Triple Crown on Citation;__

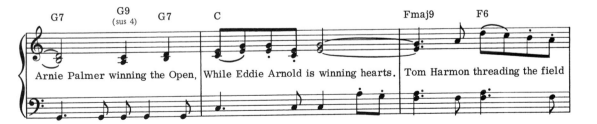

Arnie Palmer winning the Open, While Eddie Arnold is winning hearts. Tom Harmon threading the field

for Michigan, While Bob Morrison plays his heart out for Troy. Kate Smith singing

"God Bless America," and Irving Berlin, who wrote it! Then there are

Interlude

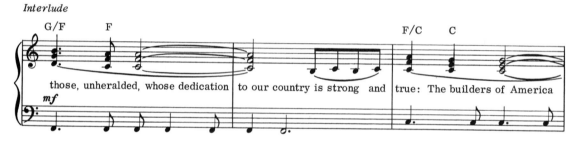

those, unheralded, whose dedication to our country is strong and true: The builders of America

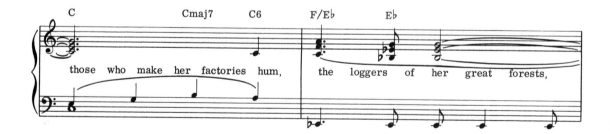

those who make her factories hum, the loggers of her great forests,

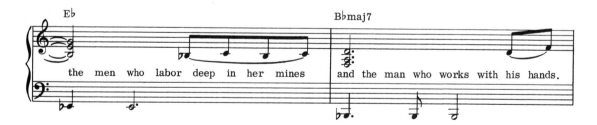

the men who labor deep in her mines and the man who works with his hands.

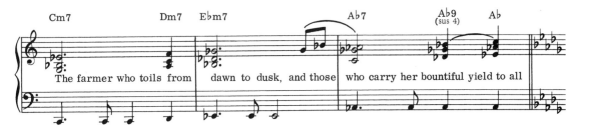

The farmer who toils from | dawn to dusk, and those | who carry her bountiful yield to all

Verse

the states of our Union. | The railroaders, our merchant | sailors, the airline pilots and those

modern knights of the road... | the truck drivers. | These, and others

like them, have earned their right to | walk proudly... with the

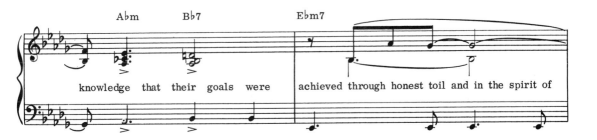

knowledge that their goals were | achieved through honest toil and in the spirit of

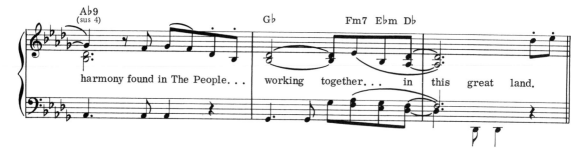

harmony found in The People. . . working together. . . in this great land.

Chorus

(Sung) What makes the word "A - mer-i-ca" ring__ with a sound that bright-ens the air?__

It's peo-ple, her peo-ple, who have done their "own thing"__ With

blood, sweat and tears, and a pray'r._____

What makes the word "America" ring
With a sound that brightens the air?
It's people, her people,
Who have done their "own thing"
With blood, sweat and tears, and a prayer.

Louis Armstrong on a golden trumpet,
And Marian Anderson singing "The Lord's Prayer";
The savage power of Jack Dempsey,
And the quiet pride of Jesse Owens;
Merle Haggard singing "Okie from Muskogee,"
And Chet Atkins pickin' a guitar;
Bing Crosby at Christmastime,
And Charles Lindbergh crossing the Atlantic alone;

A sharecropper's son, an immigrant boy,
A hobo who rode all the rails,
The magic guitar of an ol' country boy,
A lone eagle who pioneered trails;

Sandy Koufax staring down at a batter,
While Willie Mays chants his "Say hey!"
Maria Tallchief gliding in *Swan Lake,*
While Fred Astaire dances on gossamer wings;
Billy Graham bringing God to millions,
And Jonas Salk bringing hope to the world;
Mahalia Jackson closing her eyes in devotion,
And Johnny Cash singing at the White House!

What makes the word "America" ring
With a sound that brightens the air?
It's people, her people,
Who have done their "own thing"
With blood, sweat and tears, and a prayer.

Willie Shoemaker booting Swaps home,
While Eddie Arcaro wins the Triple Crown on Citation;
Arnie Palmer winning the Open,
While Eddy Arnold is winning hearts;
Tom Harmon threading the field for Michigan,
While Bob Morrison plays his heart out for Troy;
Kate Smith singing "God Bless America,"
And Irving Berlin, who wrote it!

Then there are those, unheralded, whose dedication to our country is strong and true: The builders of America—those who make her factories hum, the loggers of her great forests, the men who labor deep in her mines and the man who works with his hands.

The farmer who toils from dawn to dusk, and those who carry her bountiful yield to all the states of our Union. The railroaders, our merchant sailors, the airline pilots, and those modern knights of the road . . . the truck drivers.

These, and others like them, have earned their right to walk proudly . . . with the knowledge that their goals were achieved through honest toil and in the spirit of harmony found in The People . . . working together . . . in this great land.

What makes the word "America" ring
With a sound that brightens the air?
It's people, her people,
Who have done their "own thing"
With blood, sweat and tears, and a prayer.

An American Boy Grows Up

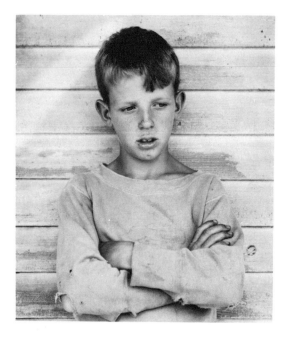

I'M taking the liberty here to expand quite a bit on this particular piece, not because I am afraid of Women's Lib, but rather because I have some daughters as well as sons and I'm very proud of them. So in my own way I'll talk about American kids growing up and I think I'll have to be qualified as an expert. I have seven of them and twenty grandchildren.

It may come as a surprise to a lot of people but a child—or children—growing up in a motion picture star's home doesn't always have such an easy way to go. Long locations tend to tear a family's ties severely and the children quite often wonder as to why it is that Dad can't stay home.

This poem means a lot to me. I don't want the "bad guys" to know it, but when it comes to children, I'm about as tough as a Boston cream pie. So it is with real feeling that I look at the words "it seems like yesterday."

How many parents there must be who remember the flush of excitement at their first born. And the slow realization that the little creature you were holding was an awesome responsibility. This child will grow up in a nation that automatically affords it the status that any other American has. *And it is the parents' job to teach that child what its nation has done for it in the past and what it expects from it in the future.*

So the children start to grow and very rapidly it becomes apparent that their personalities are very individual and often hard to cope with. Rules of conduct must be laid down and what a relief it is to be able to reach out and grab from history a quote or an event that young minds can turn to.

George Washington was reported to have said "I cannot tell a lie!" when he was a child. I've added to that and told my children if they never told a lie they wouldn't have to remember what they said. In the long run telling the truth simply unclutters your mind and you can use it to get on with what's needed to move ahead.

Personally I am in love with my country. Someone asked me a long time ago as to what I wanted for my daughters and my answer was quick and to the point: "I want them to get a good start in life." I tried to give all of my children the values that some people today call old fashioned, but most of all I want them to love their country. It's my prayer that they will never have to lift their hands to defend it but I want them to have a profound respect for those who have.

I have now watched the first four grow into adulthood. They went to school, learned their lessons well and learned to adjust, to get along with other people. It is a deep satisfaction to me that they all love America.

I watched them grow from childhood to adolescence and then into maturity. The thread that has run through all of their lives is the thread of responsibility. It has made them resolute and independent. They love their country and I love them all the more because they do.

An American Boy Grows Up

Words by
BILLY LIEBERT
JOHN MITCHUM and
HOWARD BARNES
ASCAP

Music by
BILLY LIEBERT
JOHN MITCHUM and
HOWARD BARNES
ASCAP

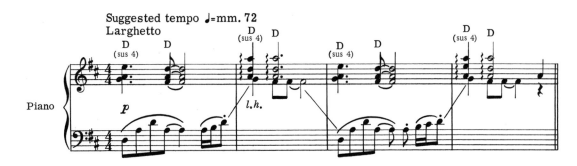

(Spoken) Our son was born so long ago,__ Yet it seems like yesterday That I stood in

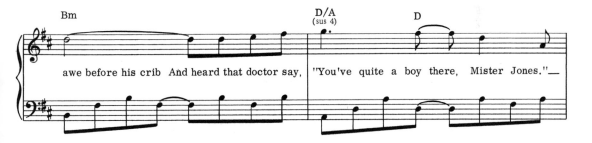

awe before his crib And heard that doctor say, "You've quite a boy there, Mister Jones."__

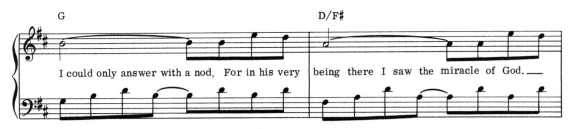

I could only answer with a nod, For in his very being there I saw the miracle of God.__

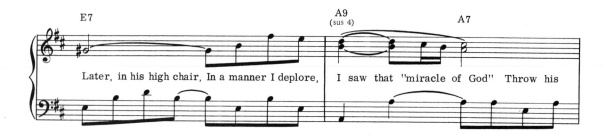

Later, in his high chair, In a manner I deplore, I saw that "miracle of God" Throw his

oatmeal on the floor.___ Well, I fixed him something different, For I felt he must be fed, But

when I turned around again, That bowl was on his head!___ A few more years rolled

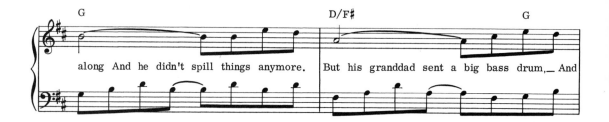

along And he didn't spill things anymore. But his granddad sent a big bass drum,___ And

once more I deplored The fact that my miracle of God Had a lusty taste for noise.___

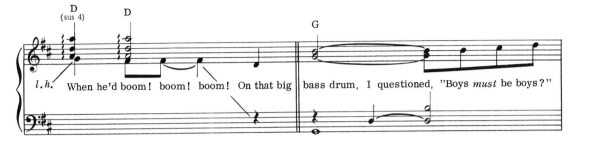

When he'd boom! boom! boom! On that big bass drum, I questioned, "Boys *must* be boys?"

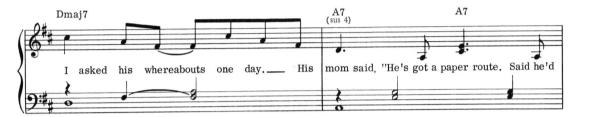

I asked his whereabouts one day.___ His mom said, "He's got a paper route. Said he'd

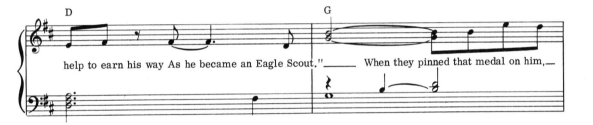

help to earn his way As he became an Eagle Scout."_____ When they pinned that medal on him,___

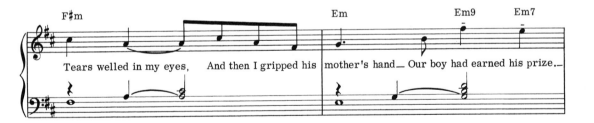

Tears welled in my eyes, And then I gripped his mother's hand_ Our boy had earned his prize._

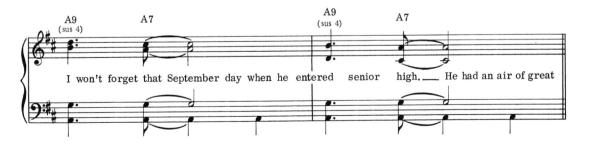

I won't forget that September day when he entered senior high.___ He had an air of great

excitement, But he left home with a sigh.___ He came back that afternoon And gave

us some puzzled looks. "Wow!" he said, "This school is tough.___ Look at all these books!"

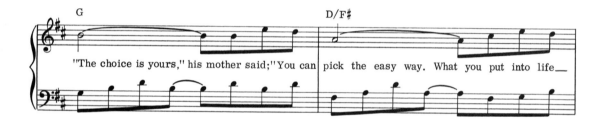

"The choice is yours," his mother said;"You can pick the easy way. What you put into life___

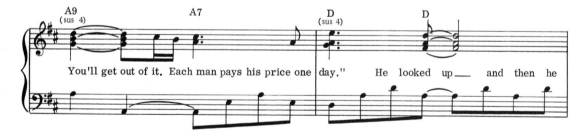

You'll get out of it. Each man pays his price one day." He looked up___ and then he

smiled,___ And I saw he'd lost his gloom. He said, "I'd better look at these." And he headed

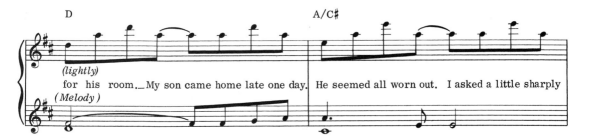

D   **A/C#**

(lightly) for his room.__My son came home late one day. He seemed all worn out. I asked a little sharply
(Melody)

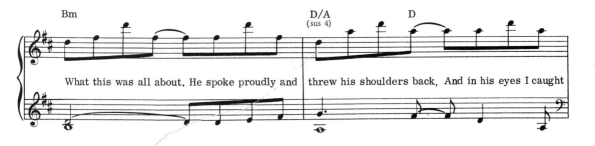

Bm   **D/A** **D**
           (sus 4)

What this was all about. He spoke proudly and threw his shoulders back, And in his eyes I caught

G   **D/F#**

a gleam. "I wanted to surprise you, Dad:____ I'm on the football team!"

E7   **A7**   **A7**
         (sus 4)

They won most of their games____ lost a few__ It was a thrill to watch him play. And when

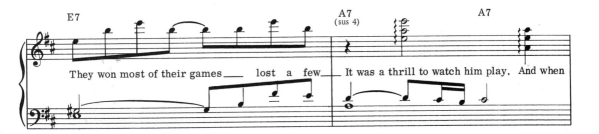

D   **A/C#**

they didn't win, we knew He'd met the challenge anyway.__He didn't know it at the time, But it

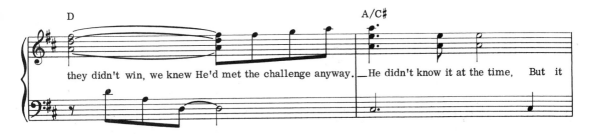

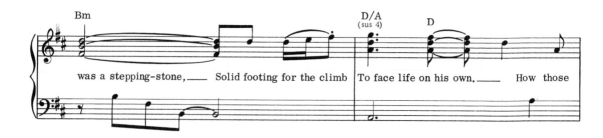

Bm / D/A (sus 4) / D

was a stepping-stone, ___ Solid footing for the climb | To face life on his own. ___ How those

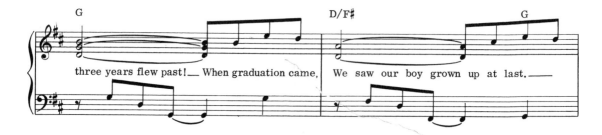

G / D/F# / G

three years flew past! ___ When graduation came, | We saw our boy grown up at last. ___

A9 (sus 4) / A7 / D (sus 4) / D

Our lives will never be the same. ___ I guess | we've known all along What his goal would

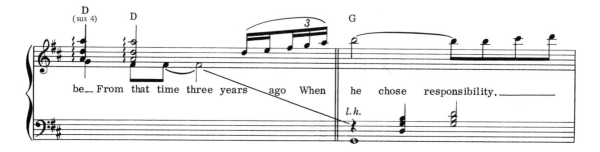

D (sus 4) / D / G

be ___ From that time three years ago When | he chose responsibility. ___

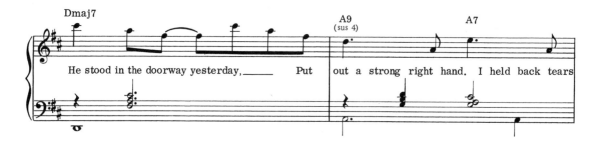

Dmaj7 / A9 (sus 4) / A7

He stood in the doorway yesterday, ___ Put | out a strong right hand. I held back tears

at the uniform He wore to protect his land.__ I shook his hand. His mother cried,

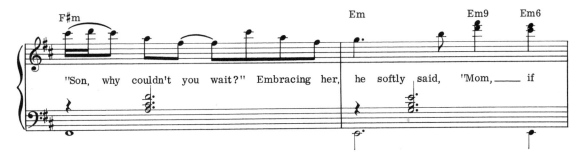

"Son, why couldn't you wait?" Embracing her, he softly said, "Mom,___ if

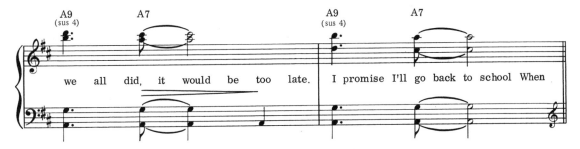

we all did, it would be too late. I promise I'll go back to school When

(lightly)
I've met my obligation__ To you,__ my friends,__ my girl,__ my school__ And most of all,__ this
(Melody)

nation. I'll do all I can out there, For I know you'll both be trying To make everyone

you know aware__ We've gotta keep Old Glory flying."__ And then his mother straightened

up.__ With a smile to hide a tear, She said,__ "We're both so proud of you! We'll feel

lost without you here.____ Someday,__ you'll know what this moment means, When

your boy shakes *your* hand____ And you watch him as he walks away.___ The

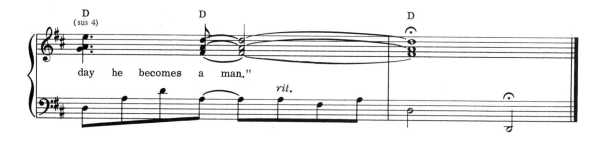

day he becomes a man."

Our son was born so long ago,
Yet it seems like yesterday
That I stood in awe before his crib
And heard that doctor say,
"You've quite a boy there, Mister Jones."
I could only answer with a nod,
For in his very being there
I saw the miracle of God.

Later, in his high chair,
In a manner I deplore,
I saw that "miracle of God"
Throw his oatmeal on the floor.
Well, I fixed him something different,
For I felt he must be fed,
But when I turned around again,
That bowl was on his head!

A few more years rolled along
And he didn't spill things anymore.
But his granddad sent a big bass drum,
And once more I deplored
The fact that my miracle of God
Had a lusty taste for noise.
When he'd boom! boom! boom!
On that big bass drum,
I questioned, "Boys *must* be boys?"

I asked his whereabouts one day.
His mom said, "He's got a paper route.
Said he'd help to earn his way
As he became an Eagle Scout."
When they pinned that medal on him,
Tears welled in my eyes,
And then I gripped his mother's hand . . .
Our boy had earned his prize.

I won't forget that September day
When he entered senior high.
He had an air of great excitement,
But he left home with a sigh.
He came back that afternoon
And gave us some puzzled looks.
"Wow!" he said, "This school is tough—
Look at all these books!"

"The choice is yours," his mother said;
"You can pick the easy way.
What you put into life
You'll get out of it.
Each man pays his price one day."
He looked up . . . and then he smiled,
And I saw he'd lost his gloom.
He said, "I'd better look at these,"
And he headed for his room.

My son came home late one day.
He seemed all worn out.
I asked a little sharply
What this was all about.
He spoke proudly and threw his shoulders back,
And in his eyes I caught a gleam.
"I wanted to surprise you, Dad:
I'm on the football team!"

They won most of their games . . . lost a few . . .
It was a thrill to watch him play.
And when they didn't win, we knew
He'd met the challenge anyway.
He didn't know it at the time,
But it was a stepping-stone . . .
Solid footing for the climb
To face life on his own.

75

How those three years flew past!
When graduation came,
We saw our boy grown up at last.
Our lives will never be the same.
I guess we've known all along
What his goal would be . . .
From that time three years ago
When he chose responsibility.

He stood in the doorway yesterday,
Put out a strong right hand.
I held back tears at the uniform
He wore to protect his land.
I shook his hand. His mother cried,
"Son, why couldn't you wait?"
Embracing her, he softly said,
"Mom, if we all did, it would be too late.

"I promise I'll go back to school
When I've met my obligation
To you—my friends—my girl—my school—
And most of all, this nation.
I'll do all I can out there,
For I know you'll both be trying
To make everyone you know aware
We've gotta keep Old Glory flying."

And then his mother straightened up.
With a smile to hide a tear,
She said, "We're both so proud of you!
We'll feel lost without you here.
Someday, you'll know what this moment means,
When *your* boy shakes *your* hand . . .
And you watch him as he walks away . . .
The day he becomes a man."

Face
the
Flag

THERE is a fad that springs up now and then in America of considering it fashionable to deplore our flag as just a symbol. Well, that's absolutely right. It is a symbol. The only fault that I can find with the pseudointellectuals who therefore discount it is that they live by symbols and apparently aren't even aware of it.

I would like to ask them a few questions. For example, why do they stop their cars when they see a red light at an intersection? It's just a symbol. The answer is obvious. The least unpleasant thing that could result from doing otherwise would be for a patrolman to give them a ticket. The God awful end result could be a screeching, tearing, rendering crash that might end with life ebbing cruelly from broken bodies. It's just a symbol, that red light, but it's wiser to pay attention to that symbol, now isn't it?

A driver going down a steep mountain road might look up to see a sign posted with lines on it depicting a dangerous curve ahead. Does that driver slow to take that curve? You bet he does. He pays attention to that symbol because it could mean life or death to him if he doesn't.

To go a step further, let's concentrate on a single dot called a period. It's always important but it can become explosive. If you should promise to pay a man $500 a week on a written contract and your secretary puts the dot in the wrong place, it could be disastrous for either party providing that they signed on the dotted line.

Think then of the symbol we call "Old Glory." It came into being by an enactment of the fifteenth Congress in 1818. Rather than go into the purely physical aspects of our flag, I will try to point out what each segment of it means in heraldry and apply it to real life situations.

Red is generally accepted to denote hardiness and valor. Washington's troops at Valley Forge surely lived up to that description just as surely as did Jedadiah Smith and Joseph Walker when they penetrated the vast mountain ranges of the West and so did the people who followed. Acts of great courage are heavily pronounced in the annals of America and they

81

most certainly didn't always take place on the field of battle. Yet, because of the fact that World War II, the Korean War and the war in Vietnam are fresh in the minds of America, there is scarcely an American who somehow, somewhere, is not acquainted with a person who once again had proved American mettle under great stress.

Remember the symbol. The red stripes on our flag represent all of America. They represent us from the dreadful winter at Valley Forge to the present and into the future. America, that is all of us, expects courage and valor from one another. It is a proud symbol and one that future generations will revere.

The white stripes in actuality represent purity and innocence. Surely the symbolism of this isn't lost on us. Despite the very real problems created by our human natures, our massive goal has always been the pursuit of justice, equality and personal happiness. To this end the often ponderous wheels of American jurisprudence seek out every avenue of truth and the American people have often asked openly if the expenditures of millions of dollars to prosecute a test case is worth the money. Emphatically yes. The search is for all of us and since those white stripes are gazed upon by millions of Americans every day, let them remember that they symbolize our constant trust to guard truth and justice vigilantly. Truth and justice that seek to be a shield for every American to carry into his daily life. A symbol? Yes, but a powerful, moving force in the constant drive toward a better world.

In the upper left-hand corner, there is a block of blue emblazoned with fifty white stars. Technically it is called the Union; it symbolizes the union of two or more peoples, incorporating their ideas and districts. Let's look at it from its real standpoint and realize that each one of those stars represents millions of Americans and that somewhere in those millions is the name you answer to.

No need to pick out a single star and say, "Hey, that's for me." Those stars represent all fifty states collectively and our founders did this with a stroke of genius. For our Union does unite two or more peoples or districts. It unites fifty districts and over two hundred million people. When you stand up and salute our flag or fly it from your home, your boat or your place of business, you are saying, "I'm grateful to be a member of that biggest Union of all, the United States of America." The color blue represents vigilance and perseverance and most certainly since revolutionary days we have epitomized those words.

So in bundling it all together we have a symbol, a symbol that for two hundred years has signified honor, valor, justice, responsibility, perseverance, hardiness and commonweal. That symbol has been the banner that millions of Americans have marched and sailed and flown with into the maws of death. They have been proud of that symbol and in turn it has slowly and patiently nurtured their common good to the extent that America stands head and shoulders over most of the world.

Yes, face the flag. It is most emphatically your flag. It has been at Iwo-jima, at the *Maine,* it has flown against the enemy in the Coral Sea and soared high in the sky above Nazi guns. Yet, it flies peacefully above every court house in the nation and stands quietly at Arlington. It is your flag, the symbol of unity, strength and honor toward you and toward your fellow Americans. Yes, face the flag, and do thank God it's still there.

Face the Flag

Words by
BILL EZELL
ASCAP

Music by
BILLY LIEBERT
ASCAP

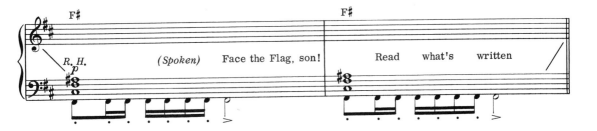

(Spoken) Face the Flag, son! Read what's written

Verse I

there,— The history, the progress and the heritage we share.—

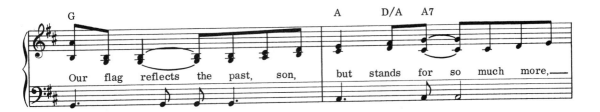

Our flag reflects the past, son, but stands for so much more,—

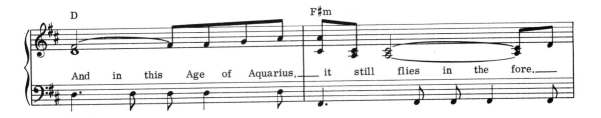

And in this Age of Aquarius,— it still flies in the fore.—

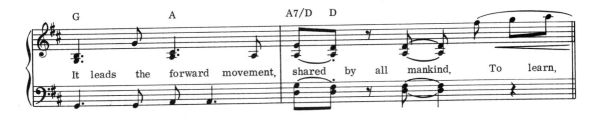

It leads the forward movement, shared by all mankind, To learn,

to love___ To live with peace of mind;__To learn the mysteries of space,

as well as those of earth;_____ To love each man for what he is,

regardless of his birth; To live without the fear of reprisal for belief;

To ease the tensions of a world that cries out for relief.

Chorus

(Sung) Face the Flag of stars and bars,__ of red and white and blue,__

A flag that guar - an - tees the rights

For men like me and you.

dim.
(as a drum beat)

(Spoken) Face the Flag, son! Take a good long look.

R. H.
p

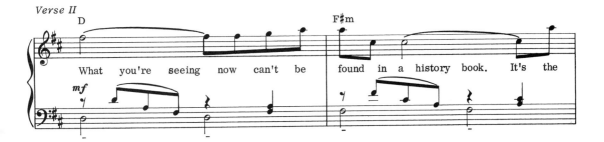

Verse II

What you're seeing now can't be found in a history book. It's the

mf

87

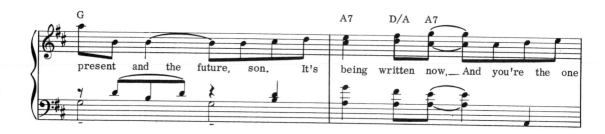

present and the future, son. It's being written now,__ And you're the one

to write it,__ but the flag can show you how.__ Do you know what it stands

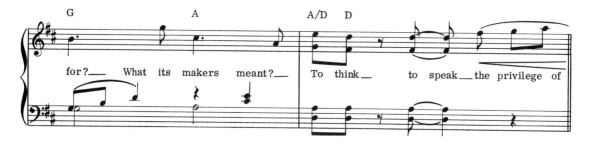

for?__ What its makers meant?__ To think__ to speak__the privilege of

dissent;__ To think our leaders might be wrong, to stand and tell them so.__These are the things that

other men under other flags will never know.__ But *responsibility*__ that's the

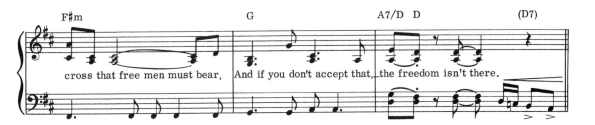

cross that free men must bear, And if you don't accept that, the freedom isn't there.

Chorus

(Sung) Face the Flag of stars and bars,— of red and white and blue,—

A flag that guar - an - tees the rights—

For men like me and you.—

(as a drum beat)

89

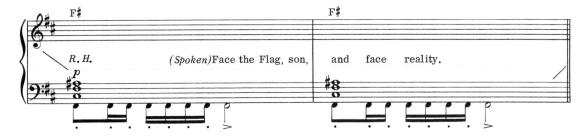

(Spoken) Face the Flag, son, and face reality.

Verse III

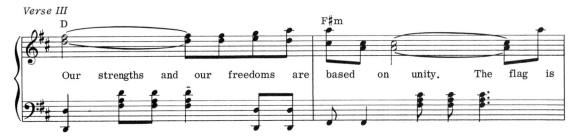

Our strengths and our freedoms are based on unity. The flag is

but a symbol, son, of the world's greatest nation, And as long as it

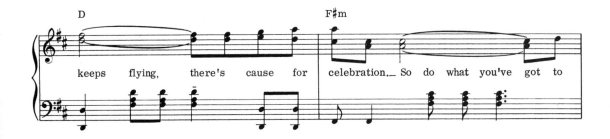

keeps flying, there's cause for celebration.__ So do what you've got to

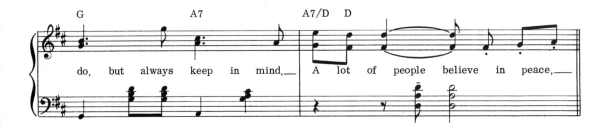

do, but always keep in mind,__ A lot of people believe in peace,__

but there *are* the other kind.____ If we want to keep these freedoms, we

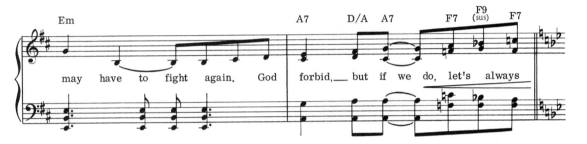

may have to fight again. God forbid,____ but if we do, let's always

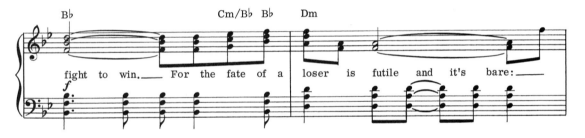

fight to win.____ For the fate of a loser is futile and it's bare:____

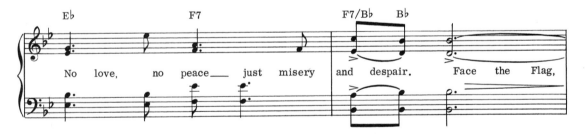

No love, no peace____ just misery and despair. Face the Flag,

son,____ and thank God it's still there.

91

Face the Flag of stars and bars,
Of red and white and blue,
A flag that guarantees the rights
For men like me and you.

Face the Flag, son! Read what's written there—
The history, the progress and the heritage we share.
Our flag reflects the past, son, but stands for so much more,
And in this Age of Aquarius, it still flies in the fore.

It leads the forward movement, shared by all mankind,
To learn . . . to love . . . to live with peace of mind;
To learn the mysteries of space, as well as those of earth;
To love each man for what he is, regardless of his birth;
To live without the fear of reprisal for belief;
To ease the tensions of a world that cries out for relief.

Face the Flag of stars and bars,
Of red and white and blue,
A flag that guarantees the rights
For men like me and you.

Face the Flag, son! Take a good long look.
What you're seeing now can't be found in a history book.
It's the present and the future, son. It's being written now,
And you're the one to write it, but the flag can show you how.

Do you know what it stands for? What its makers meant?
To think . . . to speak . . . the privilege of dissent;
To think our leaders might be wrong . . . to stand and
        tell them so.
These are the things that other men under other flags
        will never know.
But *responsibility* . . . that's the cross that free men must bear,
And if you don't accept that, the freedom isn't there.

Face the Flag of stars and bars,
Of red and white and blue,
A flag that guarantees the rights
For men like me and you.

Face the Flag, son, and face reality.
Our strengths and our freedoms are based in unity.
The flag is but a symbol, son, of the world's greatest nation,
And as long as it keeps flying, there's cause for celebration.

So do what you've got to do, but always keep in mind,
A lot of people believe in peace . . . but there *are* the
    other kind.
If we want to keep these freedoms, we may have to fight again.
God forbid, but if we do, let's always fight to win,
For the fate of a loser is futile and it's bare:
No love, no peace . . . just misery and despair.

Face the Flag, son . . . and thank God it's still there.

OURS...to fight for

FREEDOM FROM WANT

The
Good
Things

CHUCK SLADE

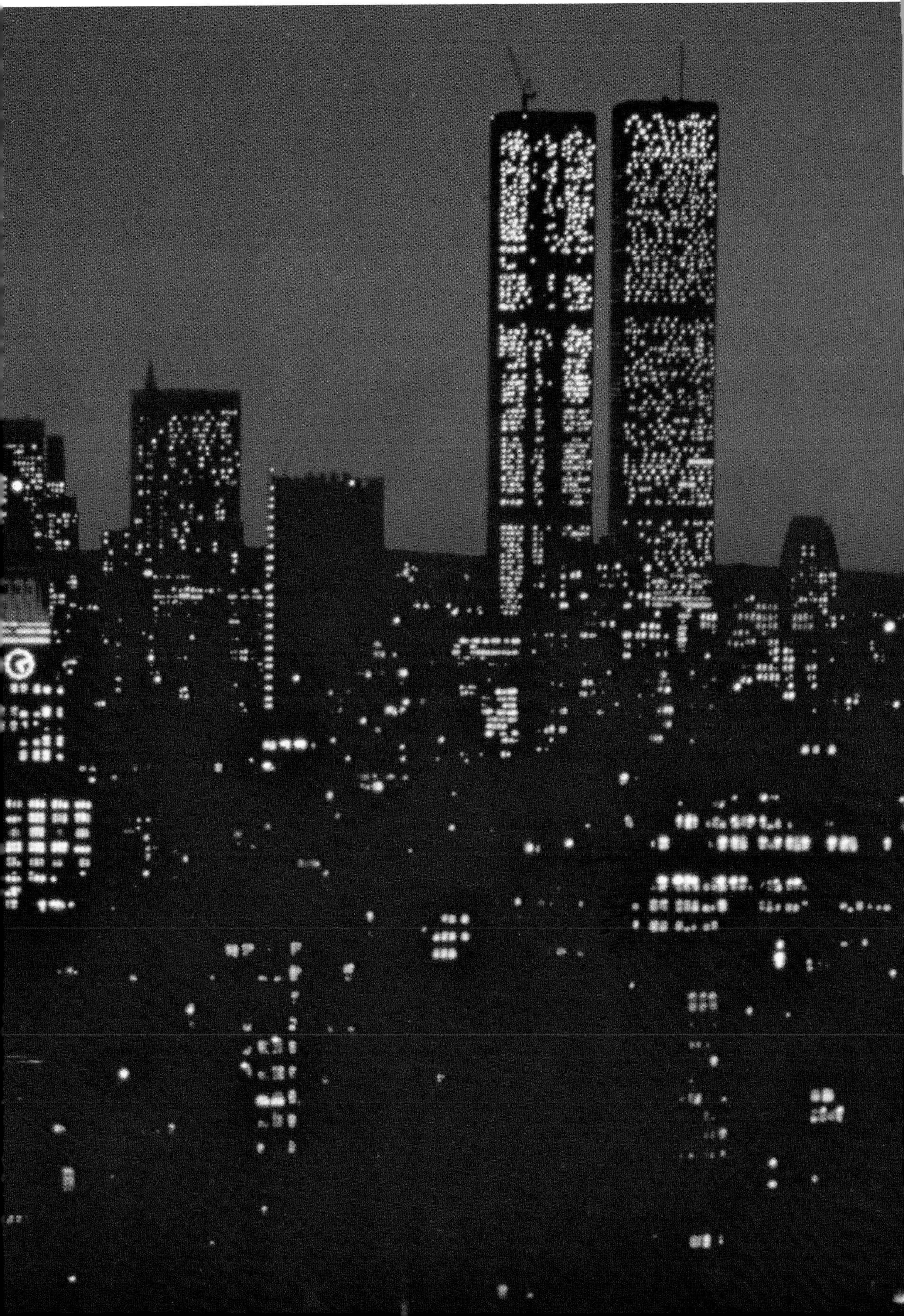

IT'S no real chore for me to write about "The Good Things" of America, although I wondered for quite a while as to why it was so hard to start. Then it came to me loud and clear. There are so many good things about America, I found myself trying to eliminate hundreds of them that I might at least not write a book on the subject. It was then that I decided to dwell upon facets of America that in each case covers a sea of individual "Good Things."

Therefore, I suppose that my number one topic should be my job. It's the one thing that takes up most of my time. It's something I'm grateful for because it's a job that I love to do. If any youngster should ask me for some advice on that subject, I'd have to tell him that he must first find out what he really wants to do with his life. Take a long hard look and make darn sure that it's what you really, really want. Then jump in feet first and give it all you have. The chances are that you'll succeed, for success is not measured in your wealth but in your worth. A person who is eager to go to his job every day is a happy man, and that's success. Once you've made up your mind about that life work, you'll find that these United States have every tool in the world to help you along.

The major factor is our free-enterprise system. Under that system you are free to pursue whatever career suits you and you have fifty states to find it in. Yes, a "Good Thing" in our country is that right to decide what you want to do with your life and where you want to do it. Free enterprise means, "do your own thing," and if you really put your heart and soul in it, you'll have a pretty fair shot at the good life.

In many parts of the world, even though you may be a national of a particular country, you have to have visas to travel in your own nation. One of our "Good Things" lies in the fact that although we solidly back states' rights in America, every citizen can be as much at home in one state as he can be in any other. A Texan can't get by pretending that he's from New York but he can live there with the same total rights any New Yorker has. A Minnesotan doesn't speak with a Mississippi drawl, but he can move to Tupelo and not create a single wave.

Yes, in America we all savor our native state and often take for granted our unassailable right to work and live in any of the others. For we basically share our entire nation together and that's another of "The Good Things" of America.

Our country thrives on change. In nature nothing is permanent. So it stands to reason that as laws change, ideologies and mores change so that society changes and that is good. When America moves slowly to a change of long duration, that change has to be for the good of the majority. If it isn't we just rare up and the next time Election Day rolls around and we want to alter that situation, our representatives start paying attention.

No guns or bombs or Army coups. Just the biggest and best weapon of them all, our right to vote. X's on paper. The ballot box, a "Good Thing."

Let's take a look at our religious beliefs. While the majority of Americans embrace Christianity, every religion of the world has found its way to our shores. Certainly we have our share of fanatics but the preponderance of Americans have a deep rooted respect for the beliefs of their fellow man. After all, was not one of our Founding Fathers' prime considerations freedom from persecution and freedom of religion?

Here all the world's religions have gathered under the vast canopy of America's skies to live and to let live in harmony. In my opinion that's a mighty "Good Thing."

Under the umbrella of all of these "Good Things" an American can live an exciting and a full life. You may vote for whom you want, pray to whatever deity pleases you, work at whatever trade or profession you really desire and live in a country that affords you every type of terrain found in the world.

Day after day in America, people enjoy the good life. It's solid and it's real. There's so much here it's easy to take it for granted and to become alarmed at the headlines that shout out disasters in bold print. Just remember that the bad news makes up less than two percent of our nation's activities. The other ninety-eight percent, a man towing a stranger's car to a garage, a neighbor caring for a sick child or a minister making a call to a dying parishioner in a driving rain doesn't make the headlines because it won't sell papers. But the "Good Things," we have them, here in America.

The Good Things

Words by
JOHN MITCHUM and
HOWARD BARNES
ASCAP

Music by
BILLY LIEBERT
ASCAP

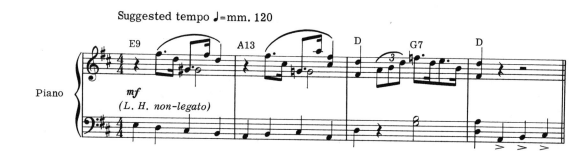

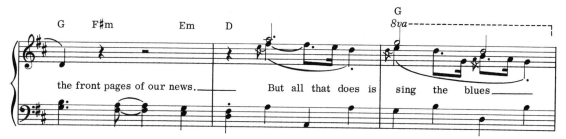

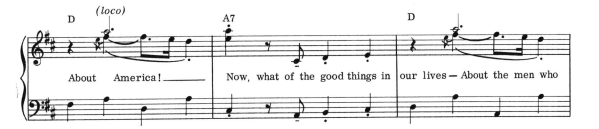

About America! _____ | Now, what of the good things in | our lives — About the men who

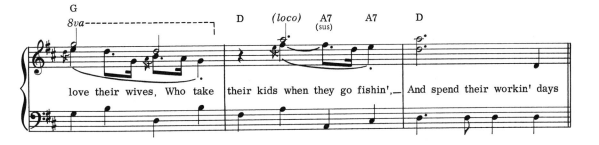

love their wives, Who take | their kids when they go fishin', _____ | And spend their workin' days

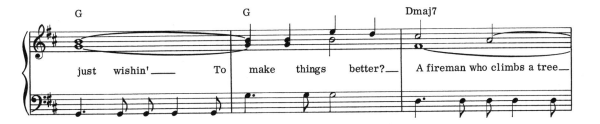

just wishin' _____ To | make things better? _____ | A fireman who climbs a tree _____

And sets a little kitten | free. _____ A | policeman who helps you cross

the avenue. _____ A | man who stops when you've | broken down And asks if you need a lift to town, _____

Or simply says,____ "Friend, what can I do?"____ Have you stopped at a

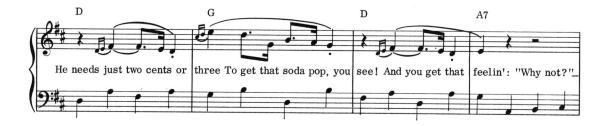

grocery store And watched a kid who's bit off more Than his five- or ten-cent piece can chew?____

He needs just two cents or three To get that soda pop, you see! And you get that feelin': "Why not?"____

And you come through.____ And how about on a Sunday morning, The sun's up high and the day is

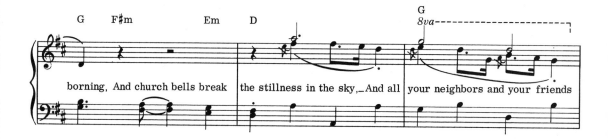

borning, And church bells break the stillness in the sky,____And all your neighbors and your friends

Climb in the family car again | And go to church,___ and | never question___ "Why"?___

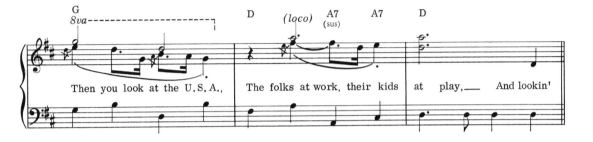

Then you look at the U.S.A., | The folks at work, their kids | at play,___ And lookin'

back, you see how hard they've | tried_To keep this country | free and strong._And | somehow you've known

all along,_The answer's here!_| Right in your own | backyard! _ For as long as | you believe in love_in

faith_ hope_ and God | above,_The future of this | land of ours is strong.__ | And most of us feel

just that way, And that's the truth!__ So let us say, "America____ can't be so very wrong!"

A ENDING*

B

* ENDING OPTIONS: 1. Play and fade (diminuendo) to silence when desired.
   2. Play themes A and B to conclusion.
   3. Omit A and play B to conclusion.

104

We hear a lot about war,
Or hurricanes that hit our shore.
We hear a lot about hard times
And a good deal more about the crimes
That make the front pages of our news.
But all that does is sing the blues . . .
About America!

Now, what of The Good Things in our lives—
About the men who love their wives,
Who take their kids when they go fishin',
And spend their workin' days just wishin'
To make things better?

A fireman who climbs a tree
And sets a little kitten free.
A policeman who helps you cross the avenue.
A man who stops when you've broken down
And asks if you need a lift to town,
Or simply says, "Friend, what can I do?"

Have you stopped at a grocery store
And watched a kid who's bit off more
Than his five- or ten-cent piece can chew?
He needs just two cents or three
To get that soda pop, you see!
And you get that feelin': "Why not?" And you come through.

And how about on a Sunday morning,
The sun's up high and the day is borning,
And church bells break the stillness in the sky,
And all your neighbors and your friends
Climb in the family car again
And go to church, and never question "Why?"

Then you look at the U.S.A.,
The folks at work, their kids at play,
And lookin' back, you see how hard they've tried
To keep this country free and strong.
And somehow you've known all along,
The answer's here! Right in your own backyard!

For as long as you believe in love . . . in faith . . . hope . . .
    and God above,
The future of this land of ours is strong.
And most of us feel just that way,
And that's the truth! So let us say,
"America . . . *can't* be so very wrong!"

A Declaration by the Representatives of the UNITED STATES OF AMERICA, in General Congress assembled.

When in the course of human events it becomes necessary for one people to dissolve the political bands which have connected them with another, and to assume among the powers of the earth the separate and equal station to which the laws of nature & of nature's god entitle them, a decent respect to the opinions of mankind requires that they should declare the causes which impel them to the separation.

We hold these truths to be self-evident; that all men are created equal, that they are endowed by their creator with inherent & inalienable rights; that among these are life, liberty, & the pursuit of happiness; that to secure these rights, governments are instituted among men, deriving their just powers from the consent of the governed; that whenever any form of government becomes destructive of these ends, it is the right of the people to alter or to abolish it, & to institute new government, laying it's foundation on such principles & organising it's powers in such form, as to them shall seem most likely to effect their safety & happiness. prudence indeed will dictate that governments long established should not be changed for light & transient causes: and accordingly all experience hath shewn that mankind are more disposed to suffer while evils are sufferable, than to right themselves by abolishing the forms to which they are accustomed. but when a long train of abuses & usurpations [begun at a distinguished period, &] pursuing invariably the same object, evinces a design to reduce them under absolute Despotism, it is their right, it is their duty, to throw off such & to provide new guards for their future security. such has been the patient sufferance of these colonies; & such is now the necessity which constrains them to expunge their former systems of government. the history of the present king of Great Britain is a history of unremitting injuries and usurpations, [among which appears no solitary fact] to contradict the uniform tenor of the rest [all of which have] in direct object the establishment of an absolute tyranny over these states. to prove this, let facts be submitted to a candid world, [for the truth of which we pledge a faith yet unsullied by falsehood]

I can well remember as a little boy standing up in my classroom every morning and reciting the Pledge of Allegiance. Shucks, I didn't know and I didn't care that the Pledge was first published in 1892 and that it was the result of a dream to have "a flag in every school." All I knew at the time was that for some doggone reason I had to hide my feelings from my classmates. The inner excitement that took over me when I clasped my hand over my heart and said "I pledge allegiance" was so great I just couldn't share it with anybody. All that I knew then was that somehow, mysteriously, I belonged. I belonged to something far too profound for my young mind to comprehend. But, I belonged. As I grew older, the mystery began to unfold. I wasn't just talking about some nebulous place a long way off, I was talking about the ground I was standing on. Ground that stretched from California to my Iowa homeland and beyond.

When I was five years old, my parents moved from Winterset, Iowa, to Lancaster, California. Imagine a five-year-old from the flat plains of Iowa being plunked down in a land that had huge mountains looming over its western rim and that stretched for hundreds of miles eastward—The Mojave Desert.

On to Glendale—high school—became involved in dramatics, football. My horizons widened, so did my love and yes my awe of my country. When I was sixteen I had a really personal feeling about a change that occurred in the "Pledge" at that time. It originally read, "I pledge allegiance to *my* flag"; in 1923 the National Flag Conference changed that to read, "I pledge allegiance to *the* flag." At sixteen I sort of took it personally that *my* flag had been deleted, until I realized that it really does belong to all of us.

Now, after having traveled extensively throughout the world, every word of that Pledge is precious to me. For hidden in its simplicity there lies a tremendous power. For our Republic stands for the innate dignity of all mankind, and our one nation, which became the United States of America at the hideous cost of the Civil War, is under God. We are indivisible and ever since 1776 all the world is aware of our hunger for individual liberty and our thirst for justice.

The next time you say those words, let your mind wander back to those days when you stood in your classrooms and recited the Pledge of Allegiance, for they were your first real commitment to your nation. Your first real step toward a bright new world.

The Pledge of Allegiance

Original Text by
FRANCIS BELLAMY (1892)
Additional Text by
JOHN MITCHUM (ASCAP)

Music by
KENNETH F. NELSON
Original Musical Arrangement by
BILLY LIEBERT

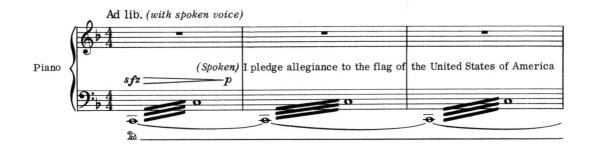

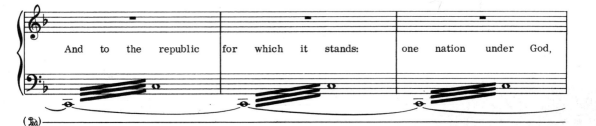

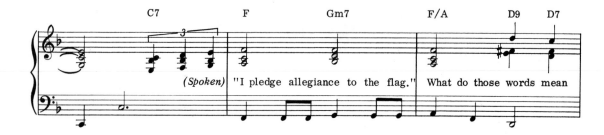

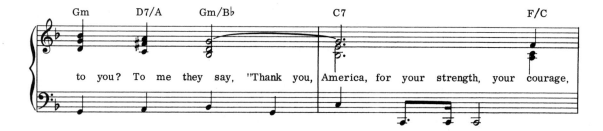

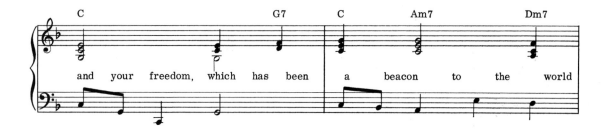

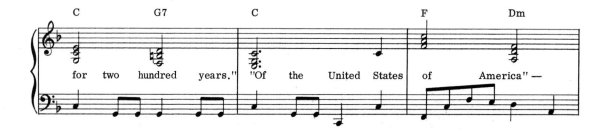

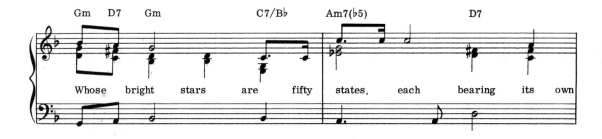

stamp of individuality, people two hundred million strong, people who have come

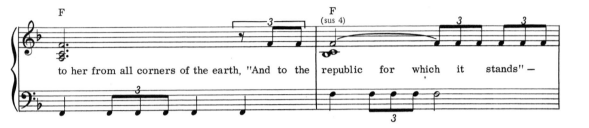

to her from all corners of the earth, "And to the republic for which it stands" —

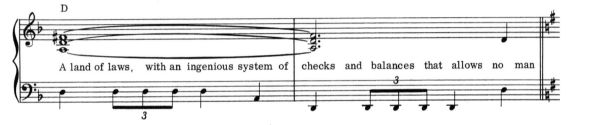

A land of laws, with an ingenious system of checks and balances that allows no man

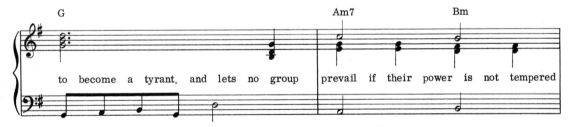

to become a tyrant, and lets no group prevail if their power is not tempered

with a real concern for the governed — A land where the

right of dissent and of free speech is jealously guarded, where the ballot box is the

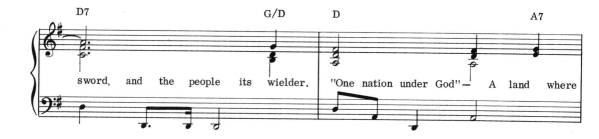

sword, and the people its wielder. "One nation under God"— A land where

freedom of worship is a cornerstone of her being — A land

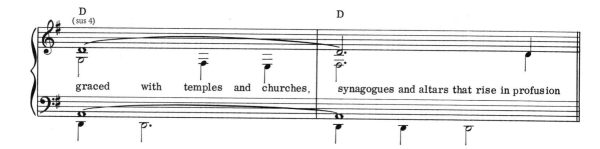

graced with temples and churches, synagogues and altars that rise in profusion

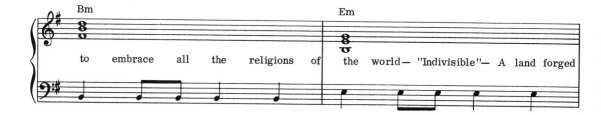

to embrace all the religions of the world— "Indivisible"— A land forged

by the hot steel of raw courage and formed forever by the awful crucible of civil war—

"With liberty"— where man in pursuit of an honest life will not be denied

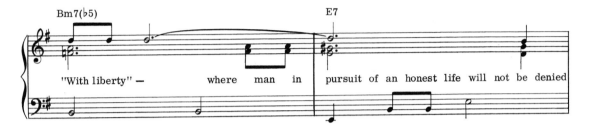

his chance, where her citizens move freely within her vast borders without hindrance or fear;

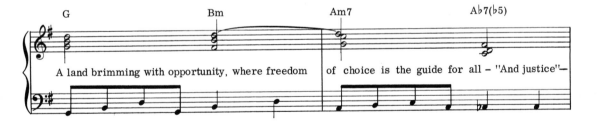

A land brimming with opportunity, where freedom of choice is the guide for all—"And justice"—

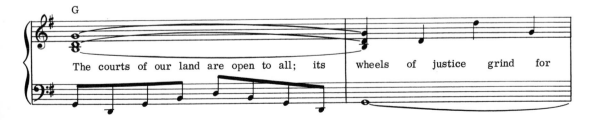

The courts of our land are open to all; its wheels of justice grind for

all causes, all people. They look to every avenue

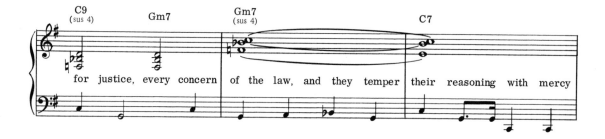

for justice, every concern of the law, and they temper their reasoning with mercy

(Sung) I pledge al - le - giance

for all.

to the flag _____ of the U - ni - ted

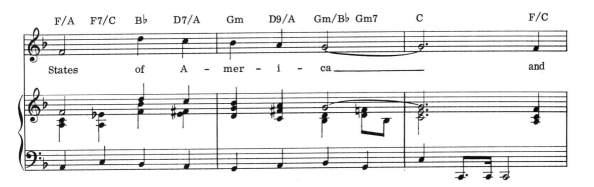

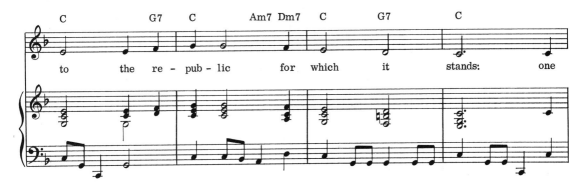

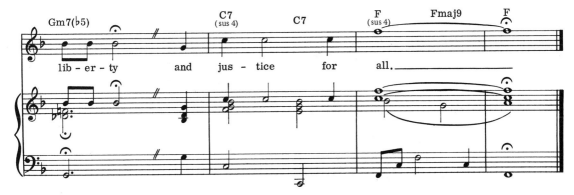

I PLEDGE ALLEGIANCE TO THE FLAG
OF THE UNITED STATES OF AMERICA
AND TO THE REPUBLIC FOR WHICH IT STANDS—
ONE NATION UNDER GOD,
INDIVISIBLE,
WITH LIBERTY
AND JUSTICE
FOR ALL.

"I pledge allegiance to the flag"
What do those words mean to you? To me they say, "Thank
you, America, for your strength, your courage and your
freedom . . . which has been a beacon to the world for
two hundred years."

"Of the United States of America"
Whose bright stars are fifty states . . . each bearing its own
stamp of individuality. People . . . two hundred
        million strong . . .
people who have come to her from all corners of the earth.

"And to the republic for which it stands"
A land of laws . . . with an ingenious system of checks and
balances that allows no man to become a tyrant . . . and lets
no group prevail . . . if their power is not tempered with a real
concern for the governed . . . A land where the right of dissent
and of free speech is jealously guarded . . . where the ballot
box is the sword . . . and the people its wielder.

"One nation under God"
A land where freedom of worship is a cornerstone of her
being . . . A land graced with temples and churches,
        synagogues
and altars that rise in profusion to embrace all the religions
of the world.

120

"Indivisible"
A land forged by the hot steel of raw courage . . . and formed forever . . . by the awful crucible of civil war.

"With liberty"
Where man in pursuit of an honest life will not be denied his chance . . . where her citizens move freely within her vast borders without hindrance or fear. . . . A land brimming with opportunity . . . where freedom of choice is the guide for all.

"And justice"
The courts of our land are open to all. Its wheels of justice grind for all causes . . . all people. They look to every avenue for justice . . . every concern of the law . . . and they temper their reasoning with mercy . . .

"For all!"
   (Vocal Chorus)

> I PLEDGE ALLEGIANCE TO THE FLAG . . .
> OF THE UNITED STATES OF AMERICA . . .
> AND TO THE REPUBLIC FOR WHICH IT STANDS . . .
> ONE NATION UNDER GOD . . .
> INDIVISIBLE . . .
> WITH LIBERTY . . . AND JUSTICE . . .
> FOR ALL.

Why Are You Marching, Son?

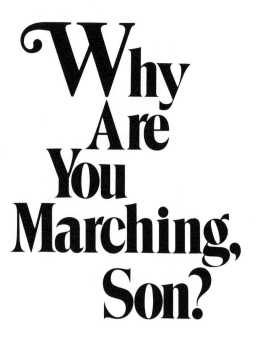

THAT'S a pretty potent question and can be answered on both sides of the fence. So when you ask it of a young rebel, he may come back with answers that run the gamut from political corruption to social unrest.

I think that a certain amount of questioning of our nation's direction and purpose is healthful, and I for one respect young people for wanting to effect change. If they don't mind however, I'd kind of like to ask them where they intend to go. If you march wildly because you want social reform and have no plan to better the social conditions that already exist, it might be better to stay home. It seems to me that a whole lot of our marches of the sixties have sure discovered that the political process of America, encompassing in its purpose the search for the best common good for all of us, may be slow and a bit tedious, but most effective in the long run.

Now if you take up arms and march for your country when she calls on you, that's a whole new ballgame. To me it means that you've already accepted the belief that your nation is on the right track for you and that you want to keep it there.

Maybe we've had "right" wars and "wrong" wars in our two-hundred-year history, and even now it's only conjectural to say how they will be evaluated a thousand years from now. But I can't help feel for example that our country wouldn't be worth much today if we would have sat back on December 7, 1941, and said, "Ah shucks, maybe we should see it from their viewpoint."

And so we marched again, just as we'd done at Valley Forge and at Belleau Wood. The millions of Americans who were transformed from fuzzy cheeked youths into formidable fighting men, marched to preserve their country and preserve it they did.

I just wish that our dissenters would recognize a darned interesting point. America didn't keep up that huge army of civilian soldiers, but in remarkably quick time returned them to civilian life. We marched when we had to and then quit marching.

Again, I'd like to ask those dissenters to think about a thing called honor. You can't put it in a sandwich and you can't hold it in your hand. You either have it or you don't and you, alone, are the one who knows. If you think it's honorable to question a commitment made by your Government to a foreign power, that's certainly your business. All I ask of you is don't consider that young boy who is fighting for you in some far-away land either a fool or a patsy. In my book, no matter how you may look at it, I feel that he's making it possible for the rest of us to enjoy the luxury of deciding to which tune we will march.

125

Why Are You Marching, Son?

Words by
JOHN MITCHUM
ASCAP

Music by
BILLY LIEBERT
ASCAP

Suggested tempo ♩=mm. 85
March tempo

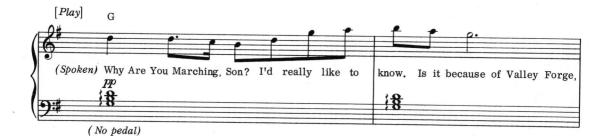

(Spoken) Why Are You Marching, Son? I'd really like to know. Is it because of Valley Forge,

or perhaps the Alamo? Or "One if by land — two if by sea," A

G   G

trumpet's call... the will to be free?   And what of a man who stood straight and tall,

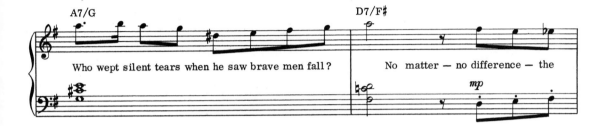

A7/G   D7/F♯

Who wept silent tears when he saw brave men fall?   No matter — no difference — the

mp

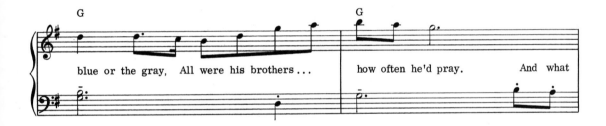

G   G

blue or the gray, All were his brothers...   how often he'd pray.   And what

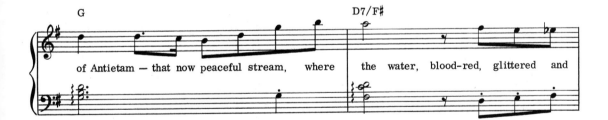

G   D7/F♯

of Antietam — that now peaceful stream, where   the water, blood-red, glittered and

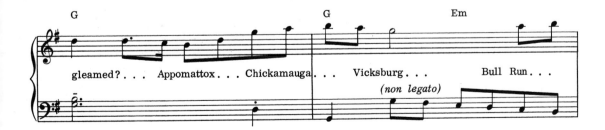

G   G   Em

gleamed?... Appomattox... Chickamauga... Vicksburg...   Bull Run...

(non legato)

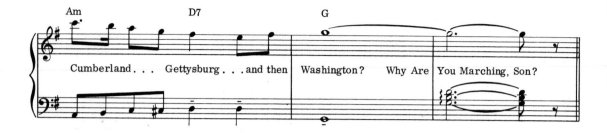

Am   D7   G

Cumberland . . . Gettysburg . . . and then | Washington?   Why Are | You Marching, Son?

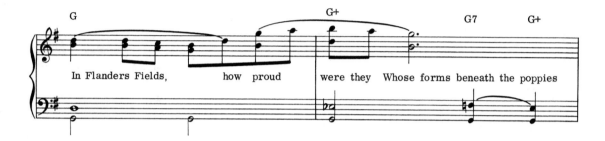

G   G+   G7   G+

In Flanders Fields,   how proud | were they   Whose forms beneath the poppies

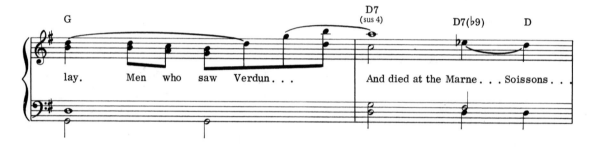

G   D7 (sus 4)   D7(♭9)   D

lay.   Men who saw Verdun . . . | And died at the Marne . . . Soissons . . .

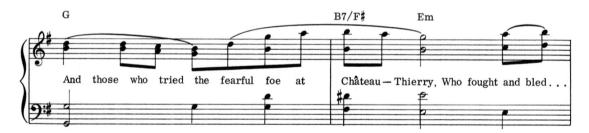

G   B7/F♯   Em

And those who tried the fearful foe at | Château — Thierry, Who fought and bled . . .

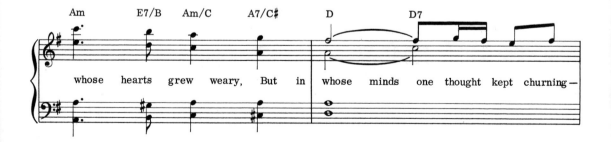

Am   E7/B   Am/C   A7/C♯   D   D7

whose hearts grew weary, But in | whose minds one thought kept churning—

That the torch of liberty keep burning.

Why Are You Marching, Son?

The planes swarmed in, and the rising sun Glowed fiercely on the evil done To men

whose blood runs through our veins, Men who died and whose remains Lie for-

ever locked in waters deep. Now, is it right that they should sleep While the warm

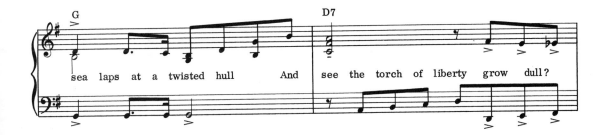

sea laps at a twisted hull And see the torch of liberty grow dull?

Anzio... Cassino... and the Po! St. Mère Église... Le Mans... St. Lo!

Gardelegen... Buchenwald... On and on the roll is called! And why?...

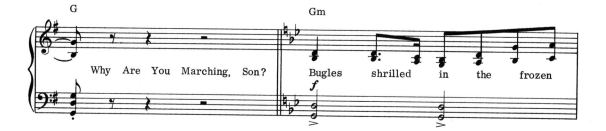

Why Are You Marching, Son? Bugles shrilled in the frozen

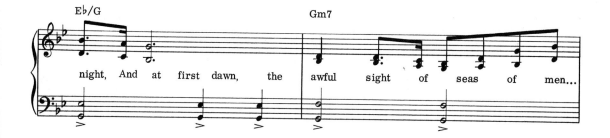

night, And at first dawn, the awful sight of seas of men...

row after row, Left to die on blood-stained snow! Pusan... Pyongyang... Suwan...

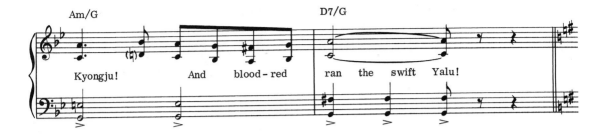

Kyongju! And blood-red ran the swift Yalu!

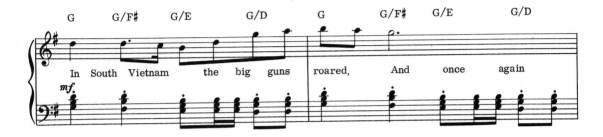

In South Vietnam the big guns roared, And once again

we fought a war To honor a pledge our nation gave To help that

little country save Her people from the certainty That she'd be ruled by

tyranny. No matter where the big guns

roar, Our fighting men, like those before, Take the torch we all hold dear

And face freedom's enemies without fear. Our fathers died from

sea to sea, And blessed the torch of liberty. Why?

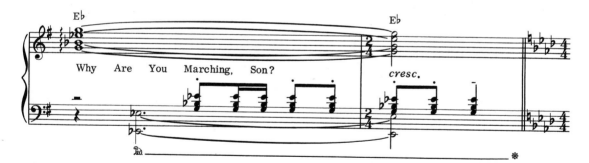

Why Are You Marching, Son?

Performance note: Fade theme if desired, or play to conclusion.

132

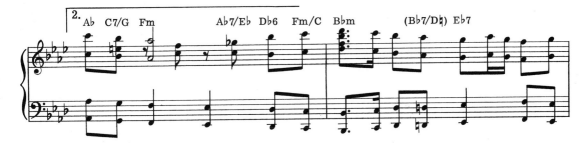

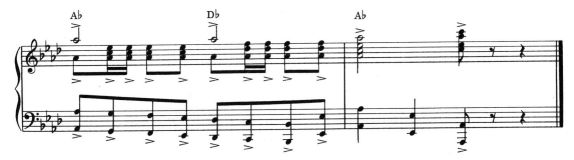

133

Why Are You Marching, Son? I'd really like to know!
Is it because of Valley Forge, or perhaps the Alamo?
Or "One if by land—two if by sea,"
A trumpet's call . . . the will to be free?
And what of a man who stood straight and tall,
Who wept silent tears when he saw brave men fall?
No matter—no difference—the blue or the gray,
All were his brothers . . . how often he'd pray.
And what of Antietam—that now peaceful stream
Where the water, blood-red, glittered and gleamed?
Appomattox . . . Chickamauga . . . Vicksburg . . .
    Bull Run . . .
Cumberland . . . Gettysburg . . . and then Washington.
Why Are You Marching, Son?

In Flanders Fields, how proud were they
Whose forms beneath the poppies lay.
Men who saw Verdun . . .
And died at the Marne . . . Soissons . . .
And those who tried the fearful foe at Château-Thierry,
Who fought and bled . . . whose hearts grew weary,
But in whose minds one thought kept churning—
That the torch of liberty keep burning.
Why Are You Marching, Son?

The planes swarmed in, and the rising sun
Glowed fiercely on the evil done
To men whose blood runs through our veins,
Men who died, and whose remains
Lie forever locked in waters deep.
Now, is it right that they should sleep
While the warm sea laps at a twisted hull
And see the torch of liberty grow dull?
Anzio . . . Cassino . . . and the Po!
St. Mère Eglise . . . Le Mans . . . St. Lo!
Gardelegen . . . Buchenwald . . .
On and on the roll is called!
134 And why? . . . Why Are You Marching, Son?

Bugles shrilled in the frozen night,
And at first dawn, the awful sight
Of seas of men . . . row after row,
Left to die on blood-stained snow!
Pusan . . . Pyongyang . . . Suwan . . . Kyongju!
And blood-red ran the swift Yalu!

In South Vietnam the big guns roared,
And once again we fought a war
To honor a pledge our nation gave
To help that little country save
Her people from the certainty
That she'd be ruled by tyranny.

No matter where the big guns roar,
Our fighting men, like those before,
Take the torch we all hold dear
And face freedom's enemies without fear.
Our fathers died from sea to sea,
And blessed the torch of liberty.
Why? . . . Why Are You Marching, Son?

THE SOLDIER BOY,
"ON DUTY"

Taps

EVER since the "Seven Day Battle" of the Civil War, "Taps" has been a part of the American way of life. The word alone became a standard and it still lingers very much on the American scene.

In my picture-making, I've done a lot of shows where the Cavalry would bed down for the night in a desert outpost. Even in a movie the sound of that lone bugle would send a shiver through me. It's funny what just a few notes can do. I've listened to some pretty complicated music in my day and some of it certainly left its impressions on me, but that simple uncomplicated strain called "Taps" tells a story that's too big for one lifetime.

How many of our heroes have gone to their final rest to its call? Heralded men whose names were household words and the unheralded, known only to God.

When you spin that tune out for over a century of time a lot of history rides on those notes. The Union's Colonel Dan Butterfield had to be a genius, for he sat down in the heat of battle, scribbled the notes down on paper and handed them to his bugler. The rest is history. Some men work for months on end putting down thousands of notes on reams of paper and unfortunately end up in obscurity. Colonel Butterfield, wanting simply to express his compassion and love for his men, captured that feeling forever with just a few notes. It seems to me that when those notes ring out, it is a melody for all Americans. God bless you, Dan.

Taps

Words by
JOHN MITCHUM
ASCAP

Original Music Adaptation and
Arrangement by
BILLY LIEBERT and
LES TAYLOR
ASCAP

139

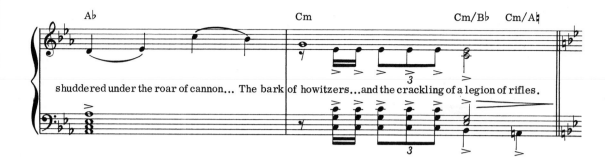

shuddered under the roar of cannon... The bark of howitzers...and the crackling of a legion of rifles.

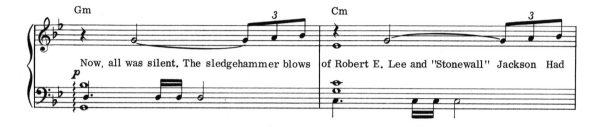

Now, all was silent. The sledgehammer blows of Robert E. Lee and "Stonewall" Jackson Had

mauled the Army of the Potomac... And yet that army was *not* destroyed. Seven thousand men had

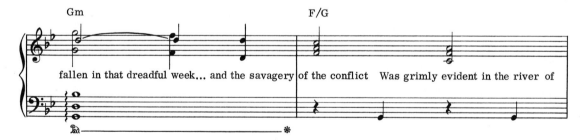

fallen in that dreadful week... and the savagery of the conflict Was grimly evident in the river of

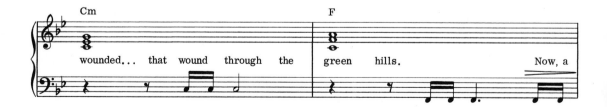

wounded... that wound through the green hills. Now, a

new sound drifted in the soft evening sky.

For Colonel Dan Butterfield, a

courageous and able soldier, Was also a man of
music. To honor his fallen comrades,

he had composed a simple and heartrending melody.
On July second, in the year 1862, Its strains

floated over the graves that scarred the dark Virginia earth.

It has been more than a hundred years since
that sound was

born...But those notes have never died away. Every night of
the year, throughout the world, fighting men of America,

From the North and the South, the East and
the West, Close their eyes in sleep to its

call. And in each of their hearts...there glows a fierce surge of pride.

Very slowly-Rubato

(Sung) Fad - ing light, fall - ing night, Trum - pet

(tre corde)

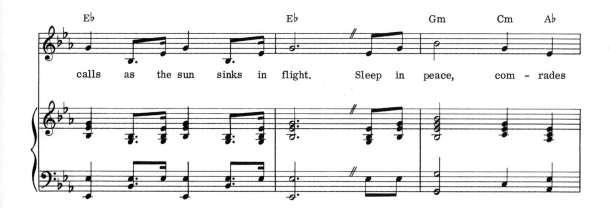

calls as the sun sinks in flight. Sleep in peace, com - rades

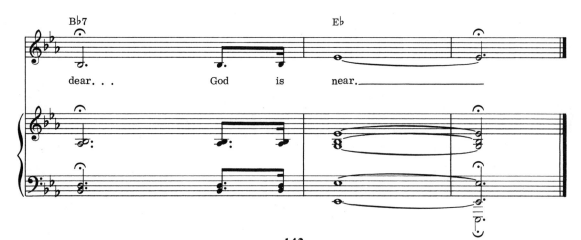

dear... God is near._____

It was July in Virginia.
The scent of the dogwood and the laurel lay heavy on the land,
While the burgeoning fruit of the peach and the apple
Marked the full sway of summer.

For seven fateful days, the trees, the flowers . . .
Yes, the very ground itself . . .
Had shuddered under the roar of cannon . . .
The bark of howitzers . . . and the crackling of a legion of rifles.

Now, all was silent.
The sledgehammer blows of Robert E. Lee and "Stonewall"
    Jackson
Had mauled the Army of the Potomac . . .
And yet that army was *not* destroyed.
Seven thousand men had fallen in that dreadful week . . .
    and the savagery of the conflict
Was grimly evident in the river of wounded . . . that wound
    through the green hills.

Now, a new sound drifted in the soft evening sky.
For Colonel Dan Butterfield, a courageous and able soldier,
Was also a man of music.
To honor his fallen comrades, he had composed a simple and
    heartrending melody.
On July second, in the year 1862,
Its strains floated over the graves that scarred the dark
    Virginia earth.

It has been more than a hundred years since that sound
    was born . . .
But those notes have never died away.
Every night of the year, throughout the world, fighting men
    of America,
From the North and the South, the East and the West,
Close their eyes in sleep to its call.
And in each of their hearts . . . there glows a fierce surge
    of pride.

"Fading light . . . falling night . . .
Trumpet calls as the sun sinks in flight.
Sleep in peace, comrades dear. . . .
God is near."